Cows to Corpses
My Life in a Village Pub

Alison Archer

Published in 2012 by FeedARead Publishing

Copyright © Alison Archer.

The author(s) assert the moral right under the Copyright, Designs and Patents Act 1988 to be identified as the author(s) of this work.

All Rights reserved. No part of this publication may be reproduced, stored in a retrieval system, or transmitted, in any form or by any means without the prior written consent of the publisher, nor be otherwise circulated in any form of binding or cover other than that in which it is published and without a similar condition being imposed on the subsequent purchaser.

British Library C.I.P.

A CIP catalogue record for this title is available from the British Library.

Front Cover Design: Peter Ware – www.17thandoak.co.uk
Website by Rob Crampton - www.cowstocorpses.co.uk

Contents

1. The Start 5
2. The Pub 10
3. The Interview 16
4. The Solicitor 22
5. The Licence 28
6. The New Chef 33
7. The New Chef Part 2 39
8. The Night Before 44
9. The Day Dawns 49
10. The First Food Night 55
11. The First Monday 61
12. End of the First Week 67
13. The Chef 73
14. The Incident 78
15. The Chef Part 2 83
16. The Drinkers 89
17. The Long, Hot Summer 95
18. The Chef Part 3 101
19. The Regulars 106
20. The Chef Part 4 112
21. The Complaint 117
22. The Winning Idea 123
23. The Chef Part 5 129
24. The Kitchen 134
25. The Bar 140
26. The Smoking Shelter 146

27. The New Regime	152
28. The Dotted Line	157
29. The Refurb	163
30. The Refurb Part 2	169
31. The Christmas Party	174
32. The Lost Licence	179
33. The Job	184
34. Christmas Day	189
35. New year's Eve	194
36. The Grumpy Man	199
37. The Pilot	204
38. The Lorry Driver	209
39. The Realist	214
40. The Older Chef	219
41. The Black Man	225
42. The Devil's Brew	230
43. The Strong Cider	235
44. The Groceries	240
45. The Customers	245
46. The Comedy Night	251
47. The News Report	257
48. The Surprise	263
49. The Husband	269
50. The First Year	274

1. The Start   February 2006

Here I am, sitting in this village pub, once again watching a man I know heave his enormous, white, naked belly on the bar counter, leaving it there to wobble gently whilst he orders a pint. I'm not sure why he does this but maybe it's to provide a little light relief for the other drinkers because his large stomach is actually quite mesmerising and I'm sure he knows it. This does illustrate quite well that country pubs are not necessarily the idyllic rural retreats you think they are. Especially this one, which I frequent on a regular basis, where the chairs are uncomfortable, the beer only passable (or so I'm told because I never drink it) and the landlord skulks up the corner refusing to speak to anyone.

All the more surprising then that my husband Rob and I love going to this pub. For all its faults it's a friendly place and has been our local since we moved to a little Herefordshire village a few years ago. We are now welcomed by name when we arrive and the farmers and other customers encourage us to sit with them to listen to idle chat or to give our opinion on any prevailing topic of conversation. In fact we love this pub so much we've decided to buy it.

I can't say owning a pub has been a life-long ambition. I'd be hard-pressed to even admit to it being a month-long ambition. But, you can't let that stop you can you? All that matters is that it seems like a good idea right at this moment. And I do enjoy going to the pub. Any pub, actually.

I first started going when I was seven years old. I say 'going', but the reality was waiting patiently outside with my younger sister. In my parents Austin

A35 van. We had a Coke and a packet of crisps each and spent most of the time trying to start the engine.

Today, if found abandoned in a van outside a pub, the social services and the police would whisk us kids away quicker than you could say, "Mine's a pint of lager", but, in the 60's it was considered quite normal and I suspect those of you who are my age, had a similar experience. It was all part of growing up then, along with Vesta curries, only having a bath once a week and watching grown men on the TV, prancing around to dance music, all blacked-up, sporting dark, frizzy, wigs. (I kid you not; this is what passed for Saturday night entertainment in those days – cavorting, lifesize golliwogs. This spectacularly un-PC extravaganza was called the Black & White Minstrel Show).

As an adult I've been going to the pub once or twice a week for years. Not to drink, because I don't much, but to enjoy the atmosphere and especially the people. Rob feels the same, although he does more drinking than me, and moving to a Herefordshire village with a local pub has fulfilled at least one of our burning ambitions.

Mind you, rural Herefordshire is not all it's cracked up to be. But, if you ignore all the squelching mud, the cowshit, the lack of shops or well-paid jobs and the fact sartorial elegance means wearing socks with your sandals, the rest is sublime.

Herefordshire is proper farming country and as of yet has been undiscovered by the vast majority of tourists. For this simple reason, it has stayed rough around the edges and there's no pressure to create anything pristine and sanitised. Which is how I consider the Cotswolds to be, all neat, straight edges controlled and contained for maximum kerb appeal. Herefordshire is a working county, full of muck and mud, of cattle and sheep, of births and deaths, of struggle and strife and above all a landscape that is a by-product of the industry that goes on in it.

In fact it's so 'country' it's said that if you look at the satellite view of Herefordshire on Google maps, when you zoom in closer a voice shouts, "Get off my land!"

Herefordshire is essentially a cider-producing county, which means lots of apple orchards with trees that are beautiful at each stage. Spindly, bare branches in the winter, fragrant apple blossom in the spring and delicious apple-heavy greenery in the late summer and autumn.

Then there are the hop fields. Herefordshire is one of the few places left in the whole country where hops are grown. The 15ft tall hop bines, grown upright on wires, intricately zigzag the fields like fine embroidery. It really is beautiful, a happy accident of its main purpose – to create a living for the farmer and the people he employs and that's why I like Herefordshire because you can see the countryside works hard for a living and fulfils a real purpose.

I've always wanted to live in the country. In the '60's, whenever we drove around in that little Austin A35 van, I coveted each and every one of the picturesque cottages we passed. Admittedly, it was difficult to see a lot because the van had no windows in the back, so my sister and I had to lean over the seats and crane our necks to look out through Mum's side window. We were all oblivious in those days to the fact that if my Dad had braked suddenly my sister and I would have hurtled through the windscreen with no child seats, or even seat belts, to prevent us. Nonetheless, the romantic glimpses I had of winding hedgerows, swaying wheat fields and vast swathes of green grass captured my heart and I was always reluctant to return to the Midlands housing estate where we lived.

Yes the countryside is wonderful and country folk (or at least the pub-goers) are 'interesting' to say the least. Take the conversation I heard in the pub the other day between two customers, one of whom was called Maurice. I knew him slightly.

"It was my wife's birthday yesterday" said Maurice

"Oh yes? Did you buy her a present?"

"I did."

"What did you get her?"

"A frying pan"

"A frying pan? Is that all?"

"It was a bloody good frying pan. It cost me the thick end of 100 quid".

Maurice's friend nodded in agreement. It certainly was expensive.

"Was she pleased?"

"No".

"Oh"

"She was even more pissed off when she opened the second present".

"Oh dear, why was that then?"

"It was a lid. For the frying pan"

So, we're buying a pub despite the fact the only experience we have is a lifetime of frequenting them. But Rob and I agree, it's time for a change. At the moment we run a graphic design and marketing business together, something we've done for 8 long years and we've really had enough. We are hoping to start new careers as Publicans by June of this year, with luck and a solicitor who's prepared to pull his finger out.

Mind you, it's going to be a challenge when we do take over. The pub is tired, run down and the drinking trade is very low. It's not going to be easy and our level of knowledge is so limited we don't even know what we don't know. What the pub does have going for it, however, is a fairly buoyant food trade and, pleasingly, no competition at all, apart from a struggling pub a mile and a half away who's landlord is like Basil Fawlty. Without the charm.

And I'm going to tell you all about it. Come what may, I'm writing this as a sort of occasional diary so you can see how we're getting on. It will either be a cautionary tale or a success story. Who knows? Like me, you'll just have to wait and see.

So, as I sat in the pub nursing half a lager, I noticed the fat man remove his gut from the counter to waddle across the bar towards the toilets. Just as he squashed through the open doorway another man appeared heading towards him. They collided and the fat man's bulk wedged them in the doorframe together. As I observed each of them trapped, struggling and straining to break free, it did cross my mind that perhaps this is a sign from which I'm supposed to take some hidden meaning? Will we get trapped in this pub we're buying? Will we be squeezed to the point of suffocation by an amorphous mass we can't control?

Then I thought, "Don't be silly. This is Herefordshire. There's nothing philosophical or metaphorical about this county. This is a plain speaking, no nonsense place where they call a spade a shovel," and where Maurice reckons a dishwasher for his wife's next birthday will make up for the frying pan he bought her for this one.

2. The Pub   Feb 2006

What I haven't told you and what I'm very ashamed to admit is the pub we are trying to buy looks so much like your archetypal little pub in the country it makes you wince.

Our pub was built in the 17th century or thereabouts (and parts of it are earlier, I believe), with a timber-frame, wattle and daub infill, multi-lit windows, a porch, a rising and falling roof and a slight lean to the left. Essentially. It's an actual black and white, old, creaky, Tudor building. I can't decide whether to be extremely smug that I'm about to realise a dream that many people can only, er, dream about or be suitably shamefaced because I'm about to live out a cliché.

In my defence, in Herefordshire there are more cosy, little black and white cottages than there are sheep, so, round here, the pub would be more unusual if it didn't look the way it does. Still, given how picturesque the pub is and how it engulfs me in waves of nostalgia every time I see it, something I find particularly compelling, I can't help wondering if my heart is ruling my head here. After all, I was the one who thought if Rob and I had been fortunate to conceive a child then the day he or she was born would be the day a rose-covered, country cottage would spring up from no-where with my name on it.

My vision of motherhood (the second time around because I already have a son who's 26) was me gently rocking a baby at the door of my little home, with my husband cooing over my shoulder and logs roaring in the fireplace behind me. I, honestly, never thought much beyond that. I can't decide if I'm just a born romantic, always looking for the best in any situation or one of life's dreamers, who is unable to see the reality, because of some infernal, rose-tinted vision.

Thankfully, sometimes, the real picture hits me in the face, before it's too late. Whilst we were trying for a baby, Rob and I went to visit a couple we knew who had just had one. We watched them, wiped out, drained, and still in their pyjamas, dog-tired from the efforts of looking after a newborn. It was like having a bucket of cold water thrown over us. Rob and I stopped wishing for a baby and went out and bought a dog instead. Much better.

At the moment, though, I still believe my little country pub is going to provide contentment and joy and nothing I've learned as of yet has persuaded me otherwise. Now listen, all of you, I'm not stupid. I know it's going to be hard work. Why do you think the Existing Landlord wants to leave? He says it's monotonous, trying, frustrating, overwhelmingly exhausting and, worst of all, your life's not your own. But, hey, that's just nitpicking. I like a challenge and now I feel alive again and, better than that, I see it as a way of making some good money.

So, the pub is quaint, idyllic and lies in a small village along with a few other black and white properties of similar period. All these ancient buildings line one side of the main (and only) street, with the pub in the middle, crowding haphazardly against each other like a mouth filled with too many teeth. Directly opposite the pub is an imposing 12th century church with an unusually separate bell tower. I don't know if this juxtaposition of God and drink was deliberate, temptation being only a stone's throw away and a test to the religious mettle of the villagers of days gone by. Or if it was a planning decision due to the lack of space. Either way, what happens now is churchgoers troop into the pub for a drink after services and a merry bunch they are too.

I think the pub is listed, but I haven't seen the deeds, so I can't tell you for a fact. I do know it's been licensed premises continuously for about the last 250 years because I found a book called 'Pubs in Herefordshire' in WH Smith and, leafing through, stumbled across an advert for our pub in the Hereford Journal dated 18th April 1776. The ad was publicising a "meeting to take place in the pub to consult about flooding in the parish' (It floods?). The book also mentions the pub used to be two houses, owned by the church. Apparently, the buildings were bought by a gentleman (of superb vision, it has to be said) and turned into a coaching inn.

As I mentioned, the building itself looks old and rickety, but very charming. The front porch leads to a tiny hallway with a door to the right and a door to the left and a hatch directly in front from where, incidentally, they used to serve itinerant hop-pickers in the '50's. In those days, the landlord wouldn't let the field hands in the pub. I think he was worried they might cause trouble or damage something when worse for wear so the workers used to queue up at this hatch, eager to buy takeaway beer. Keen to ensure his customers were well looked after, the landlord refused to supply them with glasses so, instead, the hop-pickers used to steal the jam jars and vases from the graveyard opposite to put their precious beer in. I hope they rinsed them out first.

The pub is really not very big. From the outside it's lovely and very inviting, but it's a disappointment when you get inside. If you take the door to the left, into the public bar, it's easy to see that 400 years of successive owners have not been kind to the place. I don't think there is one original feature left (apart from some of the customers of course). This is very sad. Where has the cobbled floor gone, the fireplaces, the latched internal doors and the oak panelling? Now, I realise none of these things may be remotely authentic for a 17th century, timber-frame building, but at least they would suggest a sense of close antiquity.

Instead, there are cheap orange tiles on the floor around the bar and overhead lighting so fierce, you have to shield your eyes from the glare when you enter. The pub may be characterful on the outside, with massive kerb appeal, but it's searingly bright on the inside, so dazzling it looks like an STD clinic (or so I'm told). The white glare drains everyone of colour, leaving a row of animated corpses chatting at the bar. Everything about the interior screams, inexpensive – no, that is much too soft a word – it's downright cheap, and tacky, from the white and orange woodchip on the walls to the hardboard servery painted, I'm quite staggered to report, to look like wood. Why not use actual wood?

The décor emulates that of your Nan's front room, the one she keeps for best. Copious amounts of cunning little china ornaments line every flat surface, powder blue, dralon curtains (or is it velour, I never know the difference?) that are too short, frame the windows and the previously mentioned, heavily painted woodchip covers, not just the walls, but the ceiling also, an impressive feat of decorating that is wholly pointless. Such as, putting wallpaper on the doors (like my Aunt and Uncle did, but that's another story).

The ropey furniture is not old enough to be truly interesting or new enough to be stylish, say middle to late 70's and the carpet, beyond the orange tiles, is contract flooring, usually found in offices. It is also sticky and extremely beer-stained. There's an inch of dust on the photos of the football/darts/crib teams and the only concession to the fact it's actually a pub is a few horse brasses scattered around, although why these are required pub paraphernalia is anyone's guess.

So, go back to the front hallway and take the right hand door, near the old hatch, and you'll find yourself in the restaurant, a gloomy room, again stuffed with bric-a-brac and décor that looks 40 years old. Whereas the public bar has white walls with a touch of orange here and there, every one of the restaurant walls is papered with woodchip which has been 'rag-rolled' with bright orange paint. Not only that, but the fireplace is made of orange brick and the carpet is orange. It all looks like it's been Tango-ed

The one tiny, saving facet of this whole room, like finding a jewel amidst the rubbish dump, is the roof, which has low ceilings with thick wooden beams, thankfully, left free of the heavy-duty black gloss slathered on the rest. It's here you get more than a little sense of the building's history, a tantalising glimpse into the past.

To drag you back to the present, a row or two of unframed and terribly poor, amateur paintings, created by an ever hopeful local, features on each infill panel and one of MFI's finest units, all melamine and chipboard, used as a dumb waiter, sets the whole thing off nicely.

We'll definitely have to change the décor, but we haven't got anything like the sort of money the big companies spend. It would be nice to get some opinion from the regulars before we touch anything, but it's not easy to talk to the customers at the moment because I do not wish to disparage anything the existing landlord may be responsible for, (it may have been him who rag rolled the walls orange, for instance), so I'm going to wait to see what they think once it's ours.

Nonetheless, I happened to be chatting to one of the locals I knew vaguely, in the bar last week. He asked if we were planning on doing anything with the pub when we take over and I told him, as quietly as possible, that we were going to redecorate as soon as we could. "But" and here I leaned in towards him to share a confidence "The very first thing I really am going to have to do, is get rid of those god-awful, amateur paintings in the restaurant."

The local nodded knowingly, obviously understanding exactly what I was thinking, then leaned towards me and whispered,

"My wife painted those".

Oh shit.

3. The Interview   March 2006

It's early days yet, but our sense of excitement is mounting. Rob and I are buzzing with ideas and talk about it constantly to anyone who'll lend an ear. I fear we've become pub bores and because the flow of eager and willing listeners has more or less dried up, we just discuss it now with each other. We've also spent a considerable amount of time doing what Rob calls "research' which, as far as I can tell, just involves visiting pubs. He says it'll give him a feel for what makes a successful pub and having a pint or two in each, gives him an idea of how the quality of a beer can differ from place to place.

It just sounds to me like an excuse to visit as many pubs as possible in the shortest amount of time, but I'm not one to argue. Even at the risk of becoming dangerously alcoholic. I'm prepared to do it for the sake of my new business.

What I have noticed during our "research" visits is just how much the level of customer service differs from place to place. An acceptable level of service, it seems, in some pubs, is just the ability of the bar staff to be able to tell which pump dispenses lager and which cider and in some establishments it's not even that. Many's the time we've stood at the bar and received the wrong drinks without the slightest smile or fleeting eye contact from the staff. In fact, because we are not frequent visitors, there have been many times when both the staff and the other customers have ignored us. How ludicrous is it you should have to become known in a place before you are treated with cordiality?

However, if you are a regular, the one thing guaranteed to elevate customer service from the mediocre to the excellent, and you can call me shallow if you like, is free beer. In the past, we've frequented pubs where, very occasionally, the landlord offers to buy you a pint. The feeling when this happens is one of wonder and amazement because, you see, it's not just a free drink, not just a measured amount of alcohol you don't have to pay for, oh no, it represents a thank-you on behalf of the landlord, an appreciation that you visit regularly and are a valued and treasured customer. Free beer isn't a right, don't get me wrong, but it's certainly a treat and a very welcome one at that.

At our pub, the only time the Existing Landlord has bought Rob and I a drink was on the day he accepted our offer to buy. You may think that's neither here nor there, but when you've been going to a pub for the best part of two years, buying meals and alcohol on a regular basis, routinely populating a deserted bar, and even entertaining the landlord and his two staff at our home on Christmas Day, then a free pint every now and then would be nice.

So when Existing Landlord offered to buy us a pint Rob and I were quite astounded and not a little jubilant because we used to have hushed conversations with the other few regulars, pondering on what it would take to get a drink out of a recognized tight-arse. We considered birthdays, anniversaries, birth of a baby, promotion and even, as we explained, hours of playing host at our own house but no, every one of these occasions had passed in the pub, without so much as a whiff of free beer. But, like eternal youth, we had found the secret. Offer to pay vast amounts of money to relieve him of the pub and the Landlord would design to buy you a pint. We were only given the one each, but Rob and I savoured ours as if it were nectar.

Now I'm not saying it's compulsory that all landlords should give their regular's free booze, I'm just saying it's a nice touch. As I said it shows their appreciation that you've been putting money in their tills for quite a while and is good customer service. It's also likely to bring you back in the pub time and time again; on the off chance you'll get another free pint.

Good customer service isn't difficult, but it's surprising how many businesses do not consider it to be that important. Or else, they say it is and then don't put their words into actions. Take our solicitor for example. In order to buy the pub we've picked one who's experienced in pub sales. So far, so good. He may know what he's doing but it doesn't mean he has to do it very quickly. His work philosophy is 'Why send an email when a letter with a second-class stamp will do?'

Of course, you may think, it doesn't really matter how fast the solicitor goes as long as he does it properly. But it does you see because we're not actually buying the bricks and mortar, we're only buying the lease and the goodwill i.e. the business itself and the longer this process takes increases the danger the Existing Landlord will lose interest and not work hard to keep the income at the level it is now. Do you see the need for urgency?

The pub is actually owned by a huge Pub Company (the PubCo, as we call it) who is basically a landlord to whom we will have to pay rent each week. This is quite usual, but just because a PubCo owns the building doesn't mean the business itself is part of a chain. We will have complete autonomy to run the pub in any way we see fit. We could run our establishment as a pole-dancing club for off duty nuns (with the appropriate licenses, of course) and the PubCo wouldn't give two hoots as long as the rent was paid.

However, ours is what is known as a tied-lease, which means we have to purchase all our beer, cider, lager and, unlikely as it may seem, Alcopops from the PubCo. This gives the PubCo the opportunity to charge us whatever it likes for beer because we will have signed away our right to shop around for a better price. And if we do buy beer 'out of tie' we will be heavily fined. 'Ah', I hear you say, 'How will they know?' Well there's a little device in the cellar that records the amount of beer flowing through the lines and matches it to what we have bought from the PubCo. Cunning eh? With such a natural talent for suspicion, I sometimes think this PubCo should be running the Welfare State,

If you're taking a lot of money this is not too much of a problem, but if things are tight I can see, not being able to purchase better can potentially be a right pain in the arse.

Still, that's the way it goes in this trade and it's not as if we aren't aware of the tied lease from the beginning. And on the upside we'll also be the proud owners of the ton of old tat I mentioned before that lines every surface in the place, including an old, untuned, upright piano parked outside the ladies' toilets. Happy days.

Curiously, even though it has no say in how we run the pub, we have to be vetted by the PubCo. and we had our interview today with the local PubCo representative, who is female. I'm convinced that, whilst the PubCo says it wants to see if we are forward thinking, business minded, entrepreneurial would-be tenants, what it's really interested in is; are we the sort of people who'll cobble the rent together each week?

Our interview was at another pub belonging to the PubCo in Hereford and we set out Rob and I, clutching our well researched and fully considered business plan and wearing our smartest suits. We were more than a little nervous. There was so much riding on this. What if they hated us and thought we were totally unsuitable to life in a pub? All our dreams would be shattered. We had to make as good an impression as possible, so, on the way there, Rob said to let him do the talking, because, "You know how you never say anything stupid" he said "or put your foot in it".

"Ah, sarcasm," I replied. " How unsurprising".

Now Rob and I have had a lifetime of business meetings. We are well practiced and slick, adept at working together or separately whichever is necessary. It is also true that we can bullshit for England, prepared or on the hoof. It's not a talent to boast about particularly, but it surely is useful. We're both from the advertising and marketing industry where often a designer will come up with a pretty design for a logo or corporate identity and we, as account managers, have to present it to the client with a complex and convincing, instant explanation of how we thought of it. In the trade this is known as "post-event rationalization". What we say might be a load of bollocks, but it'll sound like we know what we're talking about.

Thankfully, we didn't have to bluff or invent at all during our interview today, due to the fact we knew the pub inside out, it's location and the type of customer it attracts. We spent a happy couple of hours talking about our plans for the pub to someone who was deeply interested and who didn't squirm and shift in her seat after only five minutes.

She did let slip at one point that the PubCo does not have the power of veto in lease assignment situation such as this. So, in effect, we could have had the business acumen of jellyfish and we'd still get through and although we'd worked very hard to create the right impression, we really didn't need to have bothered too much. I didn't mind though, planning is planning after all and good in any situation. Though, what impressed me most about the PubCo representative was that she bought us a drink. Two in fact. Now that's what I call customer service.

4. Solicitors   April 2006

What is it with solicitors? Is the main focus of their day to find yet another way in which they can reduce us to spitting apoplexy? Have all the solicitors missed the point of the exercise which is to help us purchase a pub, not to get involved in some deviously legal, ducking and diving to see who can drag this out the longest and, thus, earn the most cash? It's been two months now and we don't feel any further forward than we were at the beginning. Why is it taking so long?

It's not helping that the days are passing by so quickly. We're already halfway to our deadline and there doesn't seem enough time left to do all the legal things that have to be done. Why can't all the solicitors work faster? Ours will send some contract queries to the Existing Landlord's solicitor and then several millennia go by before we get a reply. It's like waiting for my hair to grow - look closely and you can't see anything happening at all, but linger a while, then stand back and you can make out a barely imperceptible difference

It's very frustrating. We've given all the solicitors a deadline of June 1st to complete, so you can see the need for urgency. Practically on a daily basis, Rob will ring our solicitor to see if anything has occurred and when told no, will then ring the Existing Landlord, to find out if he's heard anything from his own solicitor. He usually hasn't, but invariably won't chase anything when Rob suggests it. On the very odd occasion Existing Landlord does ring up to chivvy his solicitor he usually finds the bloke's not in because he only works till 4 in the afternoon and not at all on

Friday's (Is this guy a real solicitor I wonder? Is his law degree off the Internet? It must be worth asking).

There have been times when things have been so cripplingly slow that Rob rings up the Existing Landlord's solicitor himself, but, of course, the solicitor won't talk to him (otherwise Rob'd kill him, so I can see the logic in that).

Rob says this whole process is even more exasperating than waiting for me at the supermarket till to count out exactly the right change. In coppers. When he's in a rush. Rob rang our solicitor yet again today and was told we are still waiting for a letter from the Existing Landlord's solicitor.

"Why, for fuck's sake do you insist on corresponding by letter? I can understand why you won't talk on the fucking telephone because there'd be no record of the conversation, but haven't you heard of fucking email?" is what he would have replied if he hadn't already put the 'phone down.

Rob is scarily adept at confronting people, especially on the telephone. He doesn't get all tongue-tied and forget what to say like I do. He knows exactly the points he wishes to make and always get them across. His arguments are cohesive and, often, damning, leaving the recipient no-where to hide. I'm useless at it, not just because I have trouble remembering what it is I want to say, but mostly because there always comes a stage when I can see the other person's point of view. I end up feeling positively sorry for them. It's not helpful I can tell you.

I'm also far too polite to sound off at someone, even if I really want to. Stephen Fry once said, that ours is the last well-mannered and respectful generation. And he's right. I really do have an innate inability to be rude.

I remember years ago attending a business meeting with Rob, a gathering for the self-employed for some reason or other. We found ourselves in conversation with a gent who asked Rob what we did. Rob told him about our marketing and advertising company and explained that we had developed some unique tools for gaining new business. The man then looked me up and down and deciding I definitely wasn't the brains or, even the drive, behind our operation, said to Rob, "So your wife does the books then, eh?"

And do you know what scathingly, sarcastic reply I came up with? What witty retort shot from my lips? I said "No". That was it, an inadequate - "No". Though I did console myself by flashing the double V's at the man's back when he eventually walked away. I would have sworn at him, but that would have really demonstrated what a poor, stupid imbecile I am.

So, mistakenly, I really thought that, once we'd instructed a Solicitor, all he would have to do is draw up a contract of sale and cast his expert eye over the Lease (which can't be changed by the way), explaining anything to us that was tied up in gobbledygook, of which, there's a lot. We thought it would only take a short amount of time to sort out. Boy, were we wrong. I reckon it wouldn't be any more difficult if we were negotiating the purchase of, say, a small country.

I'm trying hard to understand exactly what the hold up is and it's apparently something to do with a 'Dilapidations Report'. The PubCo, quite rightly, is worried that Existing Landlord has let the place go to rack and ruin in the two years he's been there. Existing Landlord is deeply concerned about this, mainly because, I'm assuming, he thinks an independent observer would be hard pressed to understand why

Existing Landlord would let it stay in the mess it is, if it wasn't him that caused it in the first place.

The PubCo has sent a surveyor who has compiled a list of 'dilapidations' Existing Landlord has to fix, at his own cost, before he can sell to us. As I said, he's not happy.

"The work is going to cost hundreds and hundreds of pounds" he told me.

"Really? What sorts of things have to be done?" I asked with more than a little interest.

Existing landlord reeled off a list that sounded like it'd be cheaper to knock the building down and start again.

"And they've gone into a lot of detail, so it's not as if you can do a botch job that looks good for 5 minutes"

In his dismay, I think Existing Landlord was forgetting who he was talking to. He fetched the report and read one section out to me,

"Bar – Paper to ceiling deteriorating over left hand wall – strip defective paper, prepare ceiling, apply new paper and repaint with 2 coats of emulsion" We looked up simultaneously to stare at the offending ceiling.

"Doesn't look too bad to me", I said politely, and immediately regretted it. Any work the existing landlord does now will save us having to do it in the future.

"Really?" replied the Landlord "If you don't think it's too bad then I'll argue the toss with the PubCo and get it taken off the dilaps report"

Shit. "Er, ok, if you think that's the right thing to do"

"It'll certainly save me some money" and with that, Existing Landlord handed me a copy of the report and said,

"You may as well take this and have a look see if there's anything else you don't think needs doing."
Bugger, Bugger.

"What did you say that for?" was what Rob said when I showed him the report and explained that we were meant to check to see if there was anything Existing Landlord didn't need to fix.

"I dunno, really. I was just being polite".

"Well don't in future. It'll cost us too much money".

Needless to say, when Rob had a look at the list there wasn't anything else he thought could be left and, thankfully, the PubCo rep was adamant that all work on the dilapidations report had to be carried out.

So, everything is only just crawling along, but on the upside, at least, the PubCo has approved us. Yes, we found out the other day our interview was successful and we've been deemed suitable as tenants, although I'm not altogether sure that says much. As you know, it can't actually refuse anyone and has to allow the dribbling village idiot or his dog to run a pub if they want to buy a lease assignment.

In Ledbury, a small market town about 4 miles away, there's another pub owned by a PubCo. Fights are always breaking out and its become known as something of a troublespot. The police are regularly called to quell the riots and last New Year's Eve turned up about 1.00am, probably rolling their eyes and sighing at the monotonous predictability of it all, to break up a nasty fight.

The cause, the police discovered, was the landlady. She'd got absolutely rat-arsed and picked a fight with one of her customers. Who knows what the fight was about? The customer had probably made, what he thought were witty and erudite comments about her moustache. Needless to say, rather than point out in a succinct and concise manner that he was being rude, she just brained him. The astonishing thing is the customer fought back. I have met this landlady and she does, in fact, have a moustache. And she's got hairy arms and eats glass for breakfast. Honestly.

So, as the Pub Company are not too discerning about who is running its pubs, I'm not too proud of the fact we've passed muster. After all the proof of the pudding will come when we actually take over. When the business is ours, how long will it be before we either fall flat on our faces or make a roaring success of it?

At some ever-diminishing future point we may actually get to find out, but as all the Solicitors are dawdling slower than a convicted criminal walking towards the hangman's noose, who knows when that will be?

5. The Personal Licence   April 2006

Today I took a break from listening to Rob screaming at solicitors whilst gnashing my teeth in the background and went to take my Personal Licence exam.

The last time I sat an exam was around the time I was still able to wear short skirts and look virginal, obviously a long time ago, so I was a little nervous about the whole process, I can tell you.   But   Rob, who'd done his Personal Licence exam previously and is also known for having a big head (to be fair, that's literally, not figuratively. Buying hats for him is a nightmare), says for him it was easy peasy. He pointed out to me that the test is based solely on multiple-choice answers. So there I was worrying this exam would be like taking a Degree or an A level or even a GCSE, when in fact it is more like filling out a magazine quiz.

You may be unaware, but the Licensing Laws changed in 2004, the two most significant changes being that licensed premises could stay open for 24hours and that publicans now have 10 year personal licenses that allow the holders to authorise the sale and supply of alcohol. At the time, the opportunity to drink in pubs all day and all night was greeted with the same amount of rapture displayed by Rob when faced with a pile of wood, a couple of nails and a half formed plan of how to extend his shed. That is - a lot. Most pubs, though, faced with the expense and trouble of opening 24 hours a day, 7 days a week, just settled for half an hour or so extra serving time on the end of the evening or, perhaps, staying open in the afternoon.

So, in order to be able to run my pub and, most crucially, be able to sell alcohol, I need a Personal

Licence, to be gained only by passing an exam and thereby demonstrating I have a keen grasp of the new Licensing Laws. And an awareness of my social responsibilities, of course.

Sounds really important doesn't it? Well, it's not.

Rob told me the exam is based on a 92-page handbook, parts of which you learn during a one-day course. You take the exam at the end, before you go home. It really does seem very easy doesn't it? And therein lies the rub. In making the whole process of obtaining a Personal Licence simple, I think a large amount of the kudos in having one is lost. A licence should bestow a certain degree of authority, responsibility and status, like, say, a police warrant card or an American Express Centurion card or, at the very least, a Blue Peter Badge. When someone reveals they hold a Personal Licence there should be an awed silence and an air of respect as if the holder is in the alcoholic equivalent of the SAS.

Am I making too much of this do you think? Possibly I am, but perhaps it's because the only legitimate power I've ever had in my life was as School Prefect and ever since I have had a hankering to be able to flash a badge of authority.

Of course, according to Rob, many of the things I learn during my 8 (at a push) hours of tuition should hold me in good stead when running our pub. Particularly something the government calls the 'Licensing Objectives'. There are four of them and we, apparently, have to promote and uphold them as part of the duties of having a Personal Licence.

The Licensing Objectives are:
The prevention of crime and disorder
Public safety

The prevention of public nuisance
The protection of children from harm

I'm struggling a bit here to see why these have been written specifically for the Licensed Trade, especially when there's no mention of alcohol in there at all. They could as easily apply to Teachers or Car Park Attendants as Publicans. Rob agrees with me, particularly as there is no clarification whatsoever of what these woolly statements mean. Rob's done the course already and is still none the wiser as to how far you have to take 'prevention of crime and disorder'. We can't decide if it means just ring the police if it all kicks off or swing into action and become, what the papers call, "a have-a-go hero". We agreed, if it came down to it, I'd do the first whilst Rob could handle the second because, possibly, his big head combined with his specs, would act as both a useful weapon and a deterrent.

We both think the last one, "The protection of children from harm", is really referring, to underage drinking. As it doesn't actually state that in the handbook Rob was given as part of his course, we can't think what else it's referring too. Of course it could mean - 'don't drop your pint on a child's head' or 'don't swear in front of them', but who really knows?

I'm sorry to bore you with all this Government detail, but I just wanted you to see how hard it is to understand what our legal duties are. The prospect, for me, of running a pub, whilst challenging, is incredibly daunting and I'm very keen to make sure I get it right. Rob says that the Licensing Objectives are specifically loose and woolly so they can prosecute you or take your licence off you for practically anything, from real, criminal activities in your pub such as drug taking in the toilets to something minor like telling a racist joke.

But then he's a cynic. And it doesn't take someone with a big head, full of brains (according to Rob) to realise that.

Worryingly it does give Joe Public more grounds on which to complain and let's face it, people who do not frequent pubs are apt to view the whole activity as distasteful as, say, lap dancing or reading The Sun. The police would have to take any grievance seriously if it contravenes one of the Licensing Objectives and, quite honestly, are there any activities particular to pubs that don't? If you've seen Maurice trying to drunkenly balance a full pint of lager on his head to the entertainment and merriment of a packed pub then you know what I mean. You could say Maurice is contravening both the Public Safety and the Prevention of Public Nuisance Objectives but, honestly, who cares if it's a good laugh? Existing Landlord told me, in a previous pub he'd had a severe rap over the knuckles from the police because the woman who lived next door had complained about loud talking. I kid you not. The police should have just said to the complainant "look sunshine you moved into a house close to a pub, what did you expect?"

Another "new" part of the legislation is that it's now an offence to sell alcohol to a person who is drunk. Yes, you did read that correctly. It would be an illegal act if I were to sell Maurice another pint after he's finally dropped the one resting on his head. And his mate can't buy him one either because that's illegal too.

The handbook actually states, "It is an offence to allow alcohol to be sold to a person who is drunk". I can immediately see a problem with this part of the legislation – how do you define drunk? How can you tell when you've progressed from just selling another pint to committing an illegal act?

As I said there's no helpful, legal definition of the terms "drunk" or "drunkenness", which means as the landlady it would be up to me to decide whether Maurice (to continue to use the poor guy as an example) is not overly pissed and more than capable of handling another pint. After all, I've seen him consume a lot of beer on numerous occasions and he's never puked it back up, not even once.

Another bloke in our pub is visibly sober when drunk. It's really; really hard to tell he's bladdered. Except, we always hear (which is an advantage or disadvantage of village life, depending on how you look at it) that afterwards he sleeps with double-baggers. I'm not sure, however, whether that sort of poor judgement would be a valid test for inebriation in the eyes of the law.

Nonetheless, an undercover policeman, who's watched Maurice consume maybe four or five or more drinks in my pub, could slap an £80 fixed penalty fine on me, if he thinks I've served a drunken punter. It's bloody ludicrous – that's what it is. It's enough to drive you to drink.

So, anyway, I went off to be lectured for a bit and tick a few boxes on a form and am now awaiting the outcome.

6. The New Chef   May 2006

Only a month to go. Time is passing in a blur and I think about this bloody pub from the moment I wake up to the moment I go to bed. I'm even dreaming about it. Or more accurately having nightmares where I'm standing behind an extremely busy bar and desperately trying to pull pints and there's no beer coming out. All the thirsty customers are enraged, calling me names and shaking their fists, like an angry mob. I swear there's even a pitchfork or two amongst the crowd. Scary stuff.

We interviewed a couple of candidates for the chef's job today. We only interviewed two because, remarkably, they were the only two that replied to our ad in the paper. I can't believe it – we are offering a head chef position with a £20K per annum salary plus bonuses and we've had two applications. Either we're not offering a good enough package or there aren't any chefs out there.

Someone did tell me there's a severe shortage of chefs, with not many graduating from catering college each year, but I didn't think the number who wanted to work with us would be that small. Perhaps it's just Herefordshire and all the graduate chefs from here are milling around outside restaurants and pubs in London like woebegone teenagers in a shopping precinct. Or perhaps this rash of celebrity chefs is putting newcomers off rather than inspiring them. I know I'd think twice if I had to spend my training being shouted at and verbally abused by the tutor. I don't know of any other profession that can get away with it except, perhaps school teaching (I'm joking, obviously – it's the kids that swear at the teachers isn't it?).

Anyway, we invited both applicants down to the pub, just after lunch, so Existing Landlord could sit in on the interviews, as he was the only one of us with any experience. We had no idea what qualities you needed to run a catering kitchen and was hoping Existing Landlord would be able to ask the necessary penetrating and searching questions to weed out the bad from the good.

Of course we hadn't left it totally up to Existing Landlord and had previously asked both candidates to come up with two courses on a fixed budget, either a starter and main or a main and pudding – their choice - to cook for us during the interview. Rob and I figured that, in this respect alone, our vast experience of eating would come in useful.

So, the first one turned up. He looked about 12 years old and was wearing eye watering amounts of aftershave and, probably, his older brother's suit, but he had at least made an effort and it was gratifying to see he understood the importance of looking smart for an interview. He also looked terrified. Now I can understand why he'd be scared of Rob, who wouldn't? Rob's neatly packaged, but has a balding head, grizzled stubble on his chin and a constant air about him that reminds me of a feisty Jack Russell. But me? I'm just a pussycat.

We took the prospective employee in to the only vaguely private part of the pub, the public bar (I told you no-one goes in there much) and settled down on the worn benches to listen what this guy had to say. Chef 1 told us he was already working in a pub the other side of Ledbury and had about 3 years' experience (started when he was 9 years old then). Talking to us, he seemed very uncomfortable, obviously unhappy to be interrogated. I tried smiling a lot, but that just seemed unnerve him further. Nonetheless, we pressed on with our questions;

"How many covers a day are you doing at the moment?"

"Er, 'bout 40"

"Is that just in the evening or lunchtime as well?"

"Evenings"

"Ok. So how many are you doing at lunch?

"'Bout 20"

"I see, 60 covers a day then. Is that in the week or just at weekends?"

"Weekends"

"So less in the week then?"

"Yes"

Honestly, it couldn't have been more painful if we'd tried to pull his teeth out.

Rob and I staggered through a few more questions about stock rotation, ordering and EHO regulations, sounding, for all the world, like we knew what we were talking about. Which was a good job really because Existing Landlord didn't utter a bloody word. Eventually, at a complete loss as to how to elicit more than monosyllabic answers out of him, we asked Chef 1 to cook and Existing Landlord trotted him off to the kitchen. We'd agreed that Existing Landlord would watch both applicants prepare the dishes and report back on their abilities, but given his lack of participation so far, I was beginning to think he was more interested in making sure nothing was nicked.

After a short wait the first course was presented to us and, boy, was this chef's food good. Rob and I ate with gusto, making appreciative noises and nodding our heads to each other in approval. The second course, which was fillet steak, was also well cooked and presented beautifully. We expressed surprise that Chef 1 had managed to include such an expensive cut of beef in what was, frankly, a laughably small budget and he told us, more articulate that he had been at any time up to that point, he knew the butcher and had blagged some off him for free. The interview went extremely well after that as the chef loosened up a bit and talked with some expertise about the meal he'd prepared for us.

He was young, I know, and not overly experienced, but I'd read somewhere that when you're looking for a chef, the main thing to concentrate on is the fact they can cook, because you can teach them everything else they need to know, but you can't give them raw talent if they just haven't got it. But Chef 1 had it in spades. His food was delicious, cooked quickly, well presented and arrived in front of us piping hot which is a big plus point for me as I abhor lukewarm food. Ok so he was very quiet and mostly vacant, but on the food front he really did tick all the boxes.

We sent him on his way with thanks and the cash to cover the food he'd bought and settled down to wait for the 2nd Chef.

Now Chef 2 was a bit older (probably 15) but turned out to be as tongue tied as Chef 1. Are we really that frightening? He was also wearing jeans and had bed hair. Not a good start in my book. However, he did relax more than Chef 1 and during his interview showed a spark of keen initiative. Not only had he been researching 16th and 17th century food for possible "relevant" dishes, he'd also created a menu of three courses within the budget we'd given him. We were impressed with his money saving and said so.

And his food tasted lovely – in fact as good as Chef 1. However, there was an unfeasibly long wait between the starter and the main course and all the food, whilst tasty, was very nearly cold.

After Chef 2 had gone we scratched our heads. What do you do, we wondered? Both Chefs could cook very well, but neither could string a sentence together longer than about four or five words. In this respect, both were uninspiring. It's a sad fact that, because Rob and I do not have a clue what we are doing, we need someone in the kitchen who's capable of being, practically, our 3rd partner. It's all very well knowing our prospective chefs can cook but they also need to be able to head up the food division, buying food, pricing menus, dealing with staff etc. etc. We need a responsible person to join our team and neither of these two fit the bill. I know I said it was important they had the talent and everything else could be taught, but we don't know anything ourselves, so who's going do the guiding and training? And to make matters worse, we don't have enough time left to hunt for more suitable prospects.

We asked Existing Landlord what he thought and after pondering for a while he gave us a piece of hugely useful information that really helped us decide one way or the other. He told us that Chef 2 could unblock drains. Honestly, I ask you. We're interviewing for a chef not a plumber. This is the unhelpful contribution of someone who doesn't want to be blamed if it all goes horribly wrong.

Eventually, after long deliberation and mainly "gut" feeling and because he'd had the edge with his piping hot food and the wearing of a suit, Rob and I decided to give the job to Chef 1. Somehow, I landed the task of telling Chef 2 we were turning him down.

God, I hope we've made the right decision. Our intuition says it's right, but what do we know? Admittedly, when Rob gave Chef 1 the good news he seemed very happy, so perhaps his reticence and monosyllabic tendencies were just interview collywobbles. All my nerve endings are screaming with the effort of hanging on to that hope, because there's only four weeks to go to the deadline.

7. The New Chef Part 2　　　　May 2006

Bugger, it's all going a bit wrong. The day before yesterday, Rob said to me,

"It's been a week and a half since we offered the job to Chef 1"

"I know. Time flies doesn't it? It only seems like yesterday we were eating his delicious food".

"No, what I mean is, I haven't heard from him since"

"Oh, were you expecting too?"

"Yes. He was supposed to ring and let me know how much notice he had to give"

"Oh, that's strange"

"Absolutely, especially as I've tried ringing him a few times and all I get is voicemail"

Yes, it appeared our new chef, Chef 1, had disappeared. We began to get extremely worried.

Chef 1 eventually contacted us yesterday, to tell us he was sorry, but couldn't take the job after all. When pressed, Chef 1 told us his existing employer had offered him more money and as he had a baby daughter to think of (what? A baby? He's only a baby himself) he was going to stay where he was. But thanks for the opportunity blah-de-blah-de-blah. Cheers mate and thanks for dropping us in it. I have the sneaking suspicion Chef 1 never wanted a job with us really and the whole object of the interview with us was to frighten his existing boss into giving him a pay rise.

So with two and half weeks to go before we open for business, we have no chef. Honestly, I've never been so nervous in all my life. The pressure is really cranking up now, as deadline date gets closer and closer. We'll have little or no spare cash in the bank once we've bought the pub, so really do need to hit the ground running and make money from the word go. And now we have no chef. I could cry.

This remaining two and a half weeks were supposed to be for costing menus, checking what we need in the kitchen, negotiating with suppliers, setting up systems and I was also hoping that our new chef would be able to spend a couple of days cooking with Existing Landlord, who manages to do 30 or 40 covers more or less by himself. I'm intrigued to know how and, more crucially, I need our new chef to know, because he'll be expected to do the same, as we haven't budgeted for any more kitchen help.

"I reckon," said Rob this morning "Celebrity chefs have got where they are today because they have little or no competition in Chef World",

"What are you talking about?"

"Well, if the two we've encountered are anything to go by, it wouldn't take a genius to rise above the ranks and be noticed"

"What are you trying to say?"

"I dunno really, just that I expected young chefs, to be a bit more gung-ho, you know, be more go-getting and ambitious"

"Are you saying the ones we've interviewed aren't?"

"I suppose I am, yes"

"That's a bit harsh isn't it?"

He shrugged his shoulders "I just thought that if I were a second wheel in a commercial kitchen at the moment, not being able to move upwards unless the Head Chef drowned in his own soup, I'd jump at the chance to take the reins of my own kitchen, stamp my own mark on the pub, and build my own reputation"

"Perhaps a job at our pub is not that great. You've also forgotten, both Chefs we interviewed were head chefs, of sorts, already."

"I know. It doesn't seem feasible does it? They never mentioned they have to work under close supervision, so two poor misguided souls are letting these Chefs loose on their businesses. It doesn't bear thinking about, does it? I somehow expected we'd have the Herefordshire equivalent of Jaime Oliver running our kitchen, someone enthusiastic, buzzing with ideas and energy."

I nodded in agreement. "We are going to have to do a lot of hand holding aren't we?"

"Yes and that's plenty more things to do we weren't expecting"

"This pub malarkey is no walk in the park is it?"

"You're not wrong".

To make matters worse, we are having trouble getting the rest of the money out of the people who are buying our existing business. We are owed a balance of £15,000, which, obviously, will be put towards the purchase of the pub. Every time Rob contacts our purchaser to find out where the money is, he gets fobbed off with "Don't worry, it's coming. I'm just waiting for….".

Rob's is very angry and frustrated with the daily grind of pushing solicitors to do their jobs and squeezing the money out of our business purchaser. So irate in fact that on the odd occasion I'm being as thick as three sheep and not grasping what he's trying to explain, he no longer thinks I'm charming and funny but annoying and difficult. In short, Rob's lost his sense of humour. But, perhaps, the simple fact the money has been unforthcoming says more about our business purchaser's inability to pay than Rob's ability to be confrontational. So he has every right to be concerned about the whole situation and needs to keep driving it on until we get to the end, because it really is not a laughing matter.

This means, however, because our graphics and marketing company is not sold yet, we've had to continue doing the work for all the clients when we were supposed to be concentrating fully on the pub by now.

Also, Existing Landlord is cheerfully carrying out repair work, as detailed in the Dilapidations Report as cheaply as possible. Of course he is. Do you really expect anything else? He mentioned the other day he is supposed to re-carpet one of the bedrooms in the living quarters upstairs. I didn't ask what had happened to the old carpet, but Existing Landlord did say that he'd got some off-cuts of the terrible contract carpeting he'd had put down in the bar and he was going to use that. Great. I also notice that he hasn't made a start on that bloody ceiling in the bar.

So, the buyer of our company is not paying, the solicitors seem incapable of carrying out even the smallest task without Rob having to contact them daily to check they've done it, Existing Landlord hasn't finished all the dilapidations and now we have no chef. With this level of pressure and stress I can safely say a nervous breakdown would be in order except that I don't have time to have one.

Rob and I discussed our cooking facility (or indeed, the lack of it) at great length and, because we have so short a time until we take over and because it would take too long to put ads in the paper and interview the tiny amount of applicants we're bound to get, we've decided to take the most embarrassingly retrograde step of contacting Chef 2 to see if a) he's still available and b) he's willing to take the job.

There's really no way of saving face here with Chef 2. It's been over a week and half since we turned him down for the job. If he's got even half a brain, he'll realise we've been let down by the successful applicant and we're now desperate, which will either put him off working with us altogether or he'll want more money. Let's hope he doesn't realise what a strong position he's in and also, if he does take the job, that once he's had a chance to familiarise himself properly with our kitchen he can speed up and, crucially, produce hotter food.

By the way, with all this chef kerfuffle going on, I forgot to tell you I passed my Personal Licence exam. As I've explained before, not much of an achievement I know, but at least I've passed. In fact it's the second test I've passed in as many days as I now have my Food and Hygiene certificate as well. Rob's also done a Cellar Management course, so he's one up on me.

Actually, even more boo-ha-sucks to me, because after all my crowing about how easy it was, I managed to get three answers wrong in my Personal Licence exam. Rob is gloating, of course, because he got 100% right. I will just have to kick him. It's the only way of shutting him up.

So, Rob contacted Chef 2 and asked him if he wanted the job. I can't tell you what excuse Rob gave for what has happened but, nonetheless, Chef 2 has said he's more than happy to take the job (and never even mentioned more cash) and will come and see us at the weekend to discuss the next stages. So that's ok then.

8. The Night Before   May 2006

After 4, tortuous months, we take over the pub tomorrow. I'm absolutely bricking it. I'm so nervous that I'm seriously beginning to wonder what the hell we've got ourselves into. I know we've run a company before, but that was a graphics and marketing business and both of us had already worked in the industry a good 10 years before we set the organisation up, so we had some idea of what was required.

The last time I felt this tense was when I had to take my driving test on September 23rd 1983. I had to pass you see, because the very next day I was supposed to drive to Morecombe for my job. There was a good chance, if I didn't get to Morecombe, I'd be sacked or, at the very least, a big black mark against my name (bosses were really hard in those days). So there was a lot riding on it. For my three-point turn I bounced forwards and backwards between two kerbs like a bullet ricocheting in a barrel. It took 36 manoeuvers to turn the car round and I was feeding the wheel through my ten-to-two hands with the same panic you'd feel if you were trying to unwind a fat garden hose in order to put out a house fire. I had sweat trickling down my face, for the first and only time in my life. Passed my test though.

Luckily my test only lasted an hour. I can't imagine the trepidation I feel now ever going away. We'll never be able to run a pub and make enough money to stop us being evicted; I have a shit memory for a start off. I can't remember people's names. And everything we attempt will be in the full glare of the public's gaze. Oh the pressure. At least there's not too much of the public that uses the pub at present. Only a small number will witness our dismal failure. And that's another thing. What if we can't increase the trade? Oh God. What were we thinking?

Is this just stage fright? Probably. Because I do know, given the choice to stop it, now then I'd say, "No, I want to carry on". It just seems such a big responsibility, especially as we'll be employing some staff (at vast expense) and we'll be faced with paying the rent week after week. And I don't know how to pull a pint.

Rob is absolutely raring to go and can't wait. Or so he says. I think the fact he can't sit still for one second means he's as anxious as me. He keeps prowling around the house, stuffing paper into black bags and then getting it out again in case there's something he needs to keep. There's a mess all over the living room floor whilst he tries to distract himself from thinking about what we are momentously embarking on tomorrow.

Bless him. He's fought so hard to get this for us, having to deal, not only with our own solicitor, but Existing Landlord's and the PubCo's aswell, through half-soaked intermediaries. He looks drained and exhausted, the poor sod. Practically everyday has been a battle, I've given him my complete moral support of course, but I understand it's not quite the same as screaming down the phone at incompetents every day. The solicitors may have typed a few letters and shuffled some paper across each other's desks but it's really Rob who's galvanized everyone into action and got us nearly to the end. I dread to think how long this whole process would have taken if he hadn't. Years probably. Existing Landlord and the PubCo should be paying Rob, not their solicitors.

Thankfully, we sorted out the Chef situation in the end and our new Chef has tweaked the existing menu so, we can carry on creating similar food to what's being served now, but with a twist of our own. The existing menu has worked well so far and bought in many diners so a little bit of me thinks "if it ain't broke don't fix it" for a while at least. I'm really in too much of a panic to think about starting a new menu from scratch but I realise our Chef will want to flex his cooking muscles at some point, so we'll have to change the menu soon. I do think, however, that it's important not to become a "gastropub".

Rob and I have talked about this at great length and, latterly with the new chef. We want a proper country pub, which means hearty and tasty food. All home-cooked dishes, nothing pre-packed or frozen. Country food with a bit of flair. I bloody hope it works. There's a pub called 'The Pot Kiln" which has been featured recently on a TV programme called "Heaven's Kitchen". Celebrity chef Mike Robinson owns the pub and the show is all about how he and his wife have been preparing the pub for opening.

It's been fascinating, but best of all, inspiring. I really would love our pub to be like his. It's all traditional and authentic with grooves in the wood panelling that has the deep, dark lustre of centuries-old craftsmanship instead of just a bit of stained and varnished pine, or worse, routed MDF. And the weathered finish of the oak dining tables is there as a result of a hundred years or so of wear and tear rather than a man with a heavy chain.

I suspect, however that not only does Mr. Robinson have a great deal more money to throw at it than we do, he also knows a lot more about food than either myself, Rob or indeed our Chef, who, at what looks like 15 years of age or so, can't really be expected to know anything (I am trying to be nice here, especially as I have extreme reservations about the guy).

Mr. Robinson can stalk and shoot a muntjac deer and then gut it, skin it, butcher it, cook it and serve it up as some delicious dish. Frankly I reckon the most we could manage at the moment is to hunt down and kill a pizza, so we really have a long way to go before we're serving up real, authentic, country food.

We've decided to not open at all for lunchtime tomorrow and there'll also be no food, only drink, served tomorrow night to give ourselves chance to settle in. During the evening session Rob wants to try out all the things he learnt on his Cellar Management Course. He's been boring – sorry – captivating me with details about cellar temperature, cask conditions, hard spiles, soft spiles, fobbing, ullage, (I'm sure he makes half these things up). Rob keeps saying to me "I can't wait to play with my pub".

I suppose I do feel a little excited too, but I'm mainly really apprehensive. What if we're crap? Rob has never even worked in a bar before, let alone run a whole pub. I've had a lifetime of waitressing, but all you're doing then is following someone else's instructions, not making up your own systems. At the very least I know I'm not likely to drop food in people's laps, having had loads of practice (at not dropping the food, rather than dropping it). I haven't worked behind a bar for a long time though. And I don't remember ever pulling a pint of real ale. Last time I worked in a bar the pints were automatically measured in halves or whole ones – how many years ago was that?

I know, I know, we should have done a bit of work in the pub beforehand, but Existing Landlord (soon to be ex – hurrah!), has been strangely reluctant to let us have a go. I'm beginning to think that, in spite of the fact it was his decision to sell, he's a little bit possessive about it all. How weird is that? So, tomorrow, we are really going in clean and green – all three of us. There's a stock take to be done in the morning whilst we wait for everything to complete and then we have to move our own stuff in. Rob says as long as we've got a bed on the first day, we should manage. I hope he's right.

By the way, the good news is that the purchaser of our old business finally paid up. Today in fact. Talk about close to the wire. Good job Rob only spoke to him on the phone and not face-to-face, because he was ready to hit him and Rob's not a man usually prone to physical violence mainly due to the fact he is only of average height and is as blind as a bat without glasses.

Anyway, I realise I'm rambling, but trying hard to take my mind off what's happening tomorrow. God, I hope I can sleep. It'll be Thursday 1st June and, I hope, the start of a new era for us. I think we should go down the pub tonight for a drink.

9. The Day Dawns June 2006

I really can't believe it's arrived – the day we bought a pub. Except that we didn't. Yep, the utterly, blithering, imbecile solicitors have ballsed it up. We were told this morning, having arrived at the pub with all our gear, our dog and the eagerness and willingness to part with a huge amount of cash in exchange for a livelihood and a home, that the PubCo does not actually own the pub. Apparently it rents the building, from another company, a small, but crucial fact that has not revealed itself in any of our dealings with them so far. The fact the PubCo is not the owner, is not actually the problem. What is, however, is that the PubCo needs the Owner's permission for us to take over the lease and, it seems, its solicitor has completely forgotten to obtain it.

Consequently, we are not allowed to take over the pub until permission is granted and this can take from anywhere up to three weeks. We are now homeless. And with no income.

" I can't believe this," said Rob. We were sitting outside in the garden on our own. It was 9 am and the sun was shining on the morning of what wasn't the first day in our pub. "The PubCo does fucking lease assignments all the time. One after another, after another. Jesus Christ, if they can create a complicated contract that screws us down for every penny you'd think they'd remember to do something easy like ask if it's ok if they give the pub to us. All they need is a simple to-do list that says at the top - Need Owner's Permission to Re-assign the Lease. Bunch of stupid, incompetent bastards."

I kept quiet. One of us ranting was enough I think.

"Fucking hell. I spent all day and night yesterday packing our stuff into the truck. I could have been drinking in the pub instead. Do you know what, I'm going to ring up those bloody bastards and tell them they can stuff their fucking pub?"

"Don't be silly".

"Don't be silly? I'm not being silly, I'm fucking livid. How on earth did the PubCo manage to forget the tiny, but massively important fact the pub is not actually theirs. Oh yes it's fine, they said. Sell your business, give up your home, pack up all your stuff, do your back in loading the gear into a truck, no problem. Just don't expect to actually move in because we don't own the pub, oh no, we're just borrowing it. Our landlord might not like it if we give it to you without asking".

"Look, just calm down. Instead of getting angry, just think about this for a moment. What are we going to do? And I don't mean in the next few days, I mean now, this minute. We've got nowhere to sleep tonight".

"Oh, I don't know. Who cares? We'll sleep in the truck"

"I'm not sleeping in the truck. There's no room and, besides, I don't like roughing it. Do we know anyone with a caravan or, better still, a spare room?"

"Oh, I don't know. I can't think about that now. All I want to do is hit someone."

"Hmm. Do you think a prison cell makes a good room for the night, then?"

"I'd feel so much better if I could bash someone. I blame the existing landlord. It's all his fault".

"How do you work that one out?"

"Well, it's his solicitor dealing with the PubCo. Surely they all knew about this some weeks ago".

"Apparently not. Now shush." I said under my breath because Existing Landlord was walking towards us across the grass.

In his own way, I could tell Existing Landlord was as upset as we were, mainly because he had great difficulty looking either Rob or myself in the eye. Rob was not polite and sat on the garden table with his arms folded, his face scrunched up in disgust and only grunting at anything the Existing Landlord said. Anyway, after a few platitudes from him and a show of sympathy from me, Existing Landlord told us he had no desire or inclination to carry on cooking and serving in the pub for a moment longer as he'd geared himself up to stopping today and is off abroad next week to visit family.

So, he's asked us if we want to take over the pub in a sort of management capacity, acting as relief managers, until the permission to re-assign comes through and we can complete properly. He proposes we run the pub, have the takings and pay the bills etc., just as if we'd bought it today, the only difference, of course, is that we haven't actually paid him any money.

Existing Landlord left us alone in the garden to have a chat and went back inside, probably to escape Rob's palpable waves of discontent. I asked Rob what he thought and helpfully, he told me the whole situation was a right bummer. I said I'd already noticed that, but wondered if he thought we should accept Existing Landlord's offer. Rob paused for a moment to think, then said

"We should. Yes. I can't see any problems with it, can you? Existing Landlord is taking all the risk with this arrangement, not us. It could actually work in our favour. If we don't like it we can just give it back and we'll still have all our cash." He pulled me towards him on the bench and gave me a big hug. "And of course, it also means you won't have to sleep in the truck tonight"

"Hmm, I think the same. Shall we tell him yes then?"

He nodded then squeezed me tight once more and we left the bench to go inside and take over a pub.

So, we paid just for the existing stock and waved goodbye to Existing landlord. After reassembling our bed (we left our other stuff in the truck to deal with tomorrow) and letting the dog sniff every inch of her new home, which took quite a while, we spent the rest of the day playing with our pub.

We'd decided to only open in the evening, just for drinks because, as we figured, we didn't really know how to serve behind a bar and trying to do food as well would push us over the edge. I had thought it wouldn't be too difficult, I mean, come on, I've watched pints being poured for what seems like forever and, given some of the bar staff we've met over the years, know you don't need many brain cells to throw at it, which is lucky really, because we ended up being really busy.

There was a moment, just as Rob unbolted the front door at 6 o'clock, when my stomach lurched and I had a flashing impulse to run away and hide, because I was so scared. What I hadn't realised, or else I'd have been even more terrified, was that I'd be so crap.

Rob tried to teach me how to pull a pint of real ale whilst we were serving customers; because he didn't want to waste too much beer pulling pints we hadn't sold. He really shouldn't have bothered. In my inexperienced hands the real ale was either flat and lifeless or just a pint of froth, made worse because the pub was so packed. We had to serve customers quickly and I tended to panic each time because nothing was turning out right. He shouted over the din as I pulled my umpteenth bad pint,

"You need to get a feel for how the ale is coming out so you can make sure the head on the top is the right size."

"Don't know what you mean", I wailed

"Get to know the beer, understand it, get a feel for it"

"Will you shut up? The only thing I can feel is that it's wet. All over my hand"

"Bloody hell woman, it's not difficult"

And with that he pushed me out of the way and with a twiddley-dee and a twiddely-da poured a perfect pint within about 5 seconds, holding it up to show me how brilliant it was, with an entirely unnecessary smug look on his face. Sometimes, I hate my husband, I really do.

I was that rubbish. Not only was I unable to pour, my hands shook with nerves so much whilst delivering pints the floor was awash. I dread to think of the amount of booze we wasted, especially as I had to pull at least two or three pints every time just to get one half-decent one.

There is only one bar, but it's situated between the restaurant and the public bar, which means it actually serves both. It's well located because you can see the restaurant from the public bar side and vice versa, but there isn't a great deal of room. Unfortunately, we had to work together in a really tight space. Rob and I had not coordinated our working movements at all and kept crashing into each other in the confined space behind the bar. So even more beer on the floor.

The evening went by in a flash and it's now 12 am. All the customers have gone and the bar looks as if it's been flooded. I haven't even emptied any ashtrays. The whole place resembles the aftermath of a teenage house party. There's bound to be a couple of sleeping kids intertwined under a pile of coats somewhere.

My body feels as heavy as lead, but my brain is buzzing. It was exhilarating; in spite of the fact a small child could probably pull a pint better than me. After half a day and one session of being open, I love this pub, even though it's not yet mine. I'm so excited that I get to do it all over again tomorrow. But first, I really do need to go to bed. Thankfully it won't be in the truck.

10. The First Food Night   June 2006

Two days in and so far, so good. We've had two busy nights in the bar and, whilst I wouldn't win any prizes for barmaid of the year, I'm getting faster at serving a round, that's for sure. I can pour a coke, make a gin and tonic and serve a glass of wine quicker than you can say 'mine's a campari and soda', which is useful, believe me when you've got a mob of thirsty customers and only a bar between you. I still have a long way to go before Rob stops tutting every time he notices me pull a pint of real ale, but I think I've got the hang of the lager and can fill a glass competently. Well, mostly.

We also asked Chef to prepare a selection of nibbles we could pass around so the drinkers could get a free "taste" of what the food's going to be like. A fair number of customers have dropped in for a drink and to sample our canapés, delicacies such as goat's cheese on small pieces of French loaf topped off with sticky, caramelised onions. I do hope the drinkers won't be too disappointed when they realise this sort of thing is not going to happen every Friday night. Still, for the next few weeks at least, I'll be able to keep the punters entertained with all the ceaselessly terrible things I can do to a pint of real ale.

Happily, and probably to the relief of the drinkers, tonight, for the first time, I took a rest from serving in the bar and turned my attention elsewhere. Because, you see, we opened the restaurant.

I had been brooding about this over the last two days, enacting, in my head, all the scenarios where it could go horribly wrong. A recurring theme was me dropping plates of food and I couldn't help be reminded of the time, years ago and during one of the many waitressing jobs I'd had, I'd dropped a bowl of steaming, creamy pasta just as I was trying to put it down in front of a customer. Incredibly, I managed to grab the bowl in mid air before it hit the edge of the table and upturned over the diner's lap. The bowl of food stayed completely intact, in spite of the fact it had travelled downwards a good foot from my one hand to the other.

The customer was most impressed at how I'd saved that bowl of food and offered me a position in the local rugby team. I laughed and nonchalantly went back to the kitchen to fetch the pot of mustard requested by another person on the diner's table. Smug as you like, I trotted back over to the table and stretched over the pasta diner to place the pot in the middle of the table. The pasta diner jumped in surprise when my arm appeared over his shoulder, knocking the pot of mustard out of my hand. It went flying in the air and a splat of bright yellow mustard landed on the front of his trousers and on the top of one of his shoes as the pot bounced it's way down to the floor. I have waitressed scores of times since and never had anything like that happen again, but you can't help worrying can you?

Tonight, on opening night in our restaurant we had 18 customers (or covers) to manage, bless them. I know that's not many, but I felt it was more than enough for us to cope with, because it was only Chef and myself who'd be serving them.

It was our own fault we had this many diners. We were victims of our own success. They must have been sufficiently impressed with the canapés over the last couple of nights to pop back in for a meal tonight. Either that or they'd all decided to come out for a good laugh at our attempt to run a restaurant with no experience whatsoever. I really wish they'd stayed away.

To start with it was fine because we only had one or two tables, but then the rest, like vultures, dive bombed us at once, and I, thoughtlessly, sat them down and took orders willy nilly, without any consideration at all of the effect my exuberance would have on the kitchen. There were people everywhere in the restaurant, or so it seemed, and because I wasn't controlling proceedings properly, throwing orders in the kitchen like confetti, the chef couldn't cope.

Consequently, meals backed-up, and I didn't realise there was any trouble until it dawned on me, as I blithely chatted and charmed the customers (or at least tried to) and rushed around clearing tables and getting drinks, that the bell for service had stopped ringing. I sidled into the kitchen to investigate and found Chef flapping around the room in a panic, the sweat, the pans and the insults flying copiously. With one glance at the order board and another at the stove it was obvious the last few tables would have to wait at least an hour before they received anything to eat.

The only way to get through it was to help Chef as much as possible and also suffer the excruciating embarrassment of explaining to the customers they were in for a long wait. I tried to smooth waters with a few free drinks and then spent the next hour racing backwards and forwards between trying to help Chef in the kitchen and schmoozing the customers in the restaurant so they wouldn't leave and spread horrible gossip about us around the county.

I was permanently frantic and hot with embarrassment, as I do so hate to let my brand new customers down. The sweat was constantly trickling its way down my back, pooling between my bum cheeks. I could have burst into tears at any point.

Thankfully I managed to keep them all seated and entertained and the food, when it eventually arrived, looked really appetising. The diners all said it was really tasty too but to be honest, they'd all waited so long and were probably so hungry they'd have thought a mangy dog tasted like foi gras. Our timings were lousy this evening. We really ballsed it up big time.

I was just about hanging onto my sanity with my fingernails when I was called back over to one of the tables, where I'd just served all four diners with a steak each. One of the gentlemen on that table had attracted my attention by waiving a steak knife in the air and shouting, "Excuse me. Miss". Not without a little trepidation I went over hoping he was only going to ask for more mustard. It turned out his steak wasn't cooked enough. He reckoned it was medium rare and he'd asked for medium. Horrified we'd got something wrong I scooped up his plate and, stopping myself from bowing really low and uttering the word 'sorry' about 70 times, rushed back with it to the kitchen.

Poor Chef was still under pressure and now had to flash fry the gentleman's steak on the chargrill as well as continuing with what he was doing. It was a real hassle and I could tell Chef was not pleased. After a few minutes I delivered the diner's plate back to his table and watched as he cut into the steak, to make sure he was happy. He beamed at me and said it was "Perfect, thank you," I thanked him graciously and began to move away, when he said through mouthfuls of chewed meat,

"Actually, I always ask for my steak cooked less. Yes. And then when it arrives medium rare I always send it back to be cooked a bit more"

What? Why? Why? Why would you make a chef cook your meal twice?

I smiled thinly at him and walked away before I gave in to the desire to shove that diner's face in his steak and scream at him that my kitchen was in meltdown, I'd made a terrible mistake in taking on a pub and that I had to ask Chef to re-do a meal he'd already done, in spite of the fact he's got other orders coming out of his ears and was liable to liquefy into a sweat spot any moment now under the pressure.

Bloody hell, it's day three and already I'm apoplectic over the petty little mind of a customer. God help me.

Eventually, after what seems like years of hellfire, it ended and it was only 10.00pm. After I'd waived the last diner away, I went to talk to Chef and told him I would come up with a system for controlling the throughput in the kitchen so that he didn't get orders all at once. As we are serving Sunday lunch tomorrow, I suppose I'll have to do it by then.

After service, I had a mound of washing up to do and as I stood there elbow deep in suds and greasy pans I thought, "I don't think I can stand this".

It was 11 o'clock by the time I'd staggered out of the kitchen in to the bar. Rob was there serving pints, bantering with the customers and generally having a really good time. I saw him enjoying himself before he saw me and I felt that flash of resentment you get when you think your other half is not pulling his weight and leaving it all to you. As soon as Rob noticed me he gave me a hug and asked me if it was as bad as I looked. I nodded, woefully and told him about my evening, as much as I could before a customer distracted him. Rob left me, so I went and sat up a corner and nursed half a lager, feeling sorry for myself, trying hard to find something to smile about, whilst I thought about the daunting prospect of having to do it all again tomorrow.

11. The First Monday   June 2006

It's been five days since we (borrowed?) the pub and to be honest with you, I'm absolutely knackered. Is it possible to be as tired as this?

Rob and I were sitting in the Public bar, in front of the empty fireplace having a cigarette. I was trying to explain to him how it felt working in the restaurant at the moment

"I can't seem to move quickly when I'm carrying plates. My brain is willing, but my body is heavy and takes an age to respond. It's like trying to waitress under water".

"Hmm. I think I know what you're saying". Rob picked up his left arm with his right and let go. His right armed flopped back down onto his lap.

"My arms don't work properly either".

Seriously, this is not much fun. Today is Monday and, thankfully, we've closed the pub this lunchtime so we can have a bit of a rest.

Ordinarily, there's so much to do. Ex-Landlord used to open at 10am every day, seven days a week. Given the fact mornings are taken up with dragging myself out of bed, clearing up from the night before, cleaning the toilets, putting the vacuum and duster round and so much more, such an early opening time is unrealistic. Ideally, the way I feel at the moment, the pub wouldn't open at all, but I realise we have to let the punters in at some point so we can relieve them of their cash.

We've agreed on a lunchtime session of 12 to 2.30pm which means there's three and a half hours in the afternoon to unpack some more of our stuff and then open the pub again at 6pm. As we don't often finish until about 12.45am each night I keep forgetting to eat and exist on crisps. Heavens, no wonder I have no energy. Annoyingly, Ex-Landlord did all this with only the same number of staff as we have (myself, Rob and Chef). We really should be coping better than this.

"We should get some bar staff," said Rob "If only for a couple of nights a week so I can have some time off"

"What? If you're getting help behind the bar, then I want some help with the washing up".

"Hmm. We'll have to think about it".

"There's nothing to think about. Ex-Landlord didn't have extra bar staff or any help in the kitchen if you remember and we haven't budgeted for it ".

"Well, you can carry on doing all the work if you like, but I think we need help"

"I think we should learn how to work the pub properly first, before we start roping in other people".

I have discovered that, whilst my talents on the waitressing side haven't deserted me, after five days behind a bar at the end of my restaurant shift, my skills are still decidedly shaky. And two new problems have presented themselves. The first is an inability to add up in my head.

Now I've never professed to be a maths genius and, to be honest, I do find mental arithmetic a bit challenging, but I've never been this bad before. Perhaps it's because, whilst I'm trying to add up in my head, I'm also trying to carry on a warm and welcoming conversation with the customer as well as serving drinks. It's doing three things at once, isn't it? I just can't do it. So what goes is the conversation, whilst I concentrate really hard on adding up and pouring beer. I do smile widely at the customer, but there's a vacant look in my eyes because I'm counting, so I'm muttering away to myself and ignoring them when they speak to me. The customer could be forgiven for thinking he's being served by a lunatic.

The other problem is Rob, who seems incapable of putting anything back in the same place he found it. I've never noticed this tendency of his before, other than when he did DIY round the house, and then it's his own stupid fault if he can't find his drill or his tape measure. When he's fixing things the only detrimental effect his absentmindedness has on me is that I have to listen to his swearing. 'DIY- Tourettes', I call it.

When we had our other business we had a desk each and, whilst his was always untidy and mine was always pristine, I never really gave any thought to what impact his slovenliness would have when you actually share the same workspace, when you need the order pad and you can't find it or the corkscrew or a pen or countless other things like that. His behaviour drives me disproportionately apoplectic. Feelings I always have to swallow in order to face my 'public' with a smile.

Anyway, back to our chat in the Public Bar…
"It could take ages before we're completely up to speed with the pub. I don't think I can wait until then before I get some help," said Rob "Otherwise I'll just have to lie down in the bar and quietly die during service".

"Surely, it'll get better. How do people run pubs for years and years if you're always this exhausted?"

"God knows".

So far fatigue is a fact of life. It was expected. What wasn't, though, is how much more expert the locals are at running a pub than either Rob or myself and how compelled they feel at every opportunity, to inform us of what we're doing wrong. Their sense of ownership is, at times, palpable. I understand the few who use the pub regularly have a vested interest in keeping the place open, but I do wish, after only 5 days of us being here, they would keep their comments to themselves. For a while at least. Would you go into a supermarket or a coffee house and trash the layout, the lack of choice or the décor to one of the poor employees? I doubt it very much. So why do people feel they have a right to do it to me? I wonder if, because in a pub you tend to know the landlord a bit better than you know the manager of your local branch of Tesco's, you feel justified in slagging off their efforts. I bet they wouldn't go into each other's houses though and ridicule the choice of wallpaper or 3-piece-suite.

One of them got more than a bit pissed last night and in no uncertain terms voiced his opinion about how crap the pub is and what we should do with it. Apart from major building work, like knocking out the back wall of the pub completely and installing a conservatory, he also said we need to change the beer, change the menu; get more staff blah blah blah. I tried to point out to him that a) The bleeding pub's not actually ours yet and b) More importantly, not having done it before we are still desperately learning how to run it, without formulating plans to change it all. I was trying to be nice, but the regular was drunk enough to be extremely opinionated and strident. Keeping a smile on my face was really difficult. But good practice, I suppose.

Really, I see their comments as direct criticism of how we're managing and it doesn't sit well. Honestly, who really likes to be working like a slave only to be told, in effect, that you are doing it all wrong? For the first time in my life I feel really out of my depth. I am unable to control even the tiniest thing.

I believe I've just grasped how to pour a pint properly and the next one is rubbish. And I've done exactly the same thing as I did before. I just can't understand it.

On the other hand, Rob and I seem to have unconsciously adopted distinct areas of responsibility, which is actually one of the few things that is working quite well. Rob runs the bar, ordering and looking after the beer etc., and I look after the kitchen (loosely), the restaurant and the finances. This means we can learn our own areas well, without having to become experts in all aspects of the business.

Rob and I have always worked well together. We've had plenty of practice at it. Our mutual support and trust is total and we do rely heavily on each other. I know Rob will do the best job he can and he knows the same of me. It's very comforting. Rob and I have always said "it's you and me against the world" and whilst I don't wish to suggest we spend our days picking fights with everyone, like that landlady in the pub in Ledbury I mentioned before, it does mean we stand firm together and face our challenges together, whatever they may be. I know this sounds twee and sentimental although, believe me, we're not ready to wear matching sweaters yet or finish each others sentences, but there's no getting away from the fact we're each other's rock. That makes us very lucky, I know.

The only downside at the moment, however, is that we're not getting to spend any quality time together. If we're not working, or unpacking a few more boxes, then we're asleep. Ordinarily we would just go to the pub to unwind, to have a bit of a laugh with each other and our mates. Now the pub just serves to stress us out further. You can't win, can you?

So, instead, as we sat there front of the fireplace, Rob flicked his cigarette stub into the open grate and gestured for me to come close. He wrapped his arms tightly around me and for a while I felt comforted.

12. End of the First Week   June 2006

Well, today is Thursday and the end of our first, official week. We're still muscle-achingly knackered and my feet feel like someone has chewed them up and spat them out, but at least I can pour a decent pint now, more often than not. Pleasingly, someone came in and asked for a bar job and, after mulling it over for a nanosecond, Rob asked her to work on Sunday and Monday nights. As the restaurant isn't open these nights both Rob and I can have a rest together. And, because we seem to employing staff willy-nilly, I've also taken on a washer-upper for Friday and Saturday nights and Sunday lunchtimes, hurrah, hurrah, hurrah.

We've bought some chickens and housed them in an old henhouse we found in the back garden, so I'm getting fresh eggs for breakfast every morning (a good breakfast is very important to me). A few people have been in each night for food, so working in the restaurant is becoming less and less daunting as each day goes by and Rob has practiced all the things he learned on his Cellar Management course under what he calls 'battle conditions', but which I think means swiftly changing a barrel during service, under pressure to get it right first time. This can be quite daunting, as you can imagine, because sod's law says the beer will always go when you've got a pub full of people waiting to be served.

If it's the lager that needs changing, Rob has to race downstairs to the cellar, turn off the gas, unscrew the coupler on the top of the barrel, move the empty one out of the way, man-handle a new one in its place, re-couple it to the pumping system, release the air out of the cellar buoy (so it fills with beer – you can check the condition of the liquid then), and turn the gas back on.

Or something like that because it all seems a bit complicated to me. The reason for the urgency is Rob has invariably left several customers waiting at the bar for their pints plus another patron will usually walk in when Rob's not there to welcome him.

Nonetheless, things are progressing and best of all – we are in the local paper tomorrow.

This last thing gives me a lot of pleasure because, as an ex-marketing person, it was worrying me that I hadn't even thought about our publicity campaign, let alone begun one. But one of the local, large farmers (large, as in - has a lot of land) dropped in for a drink last Sunday evening and told us that many years ago he'd bought a couple of Hereford bulls down to the pub to welcome the new landlord in. The farmer asked if we'd like him to do the same thing again, to carry on the tradition. I said that would be wonderful, but didn't think I'd have much time to sort it out in the near future. The farmer, bless him, contacted the newspaper himself and arranged for a photographer and journalist to visit today. How kind and thoughtful was that?

So, at 2.30 this afternoon, myself and the journalist cum photographer peered out of the public bar window to see two massive bulls lumbering up the high street in the drizzle (they weren't on their own, of course, the large farmer and his assistant were with them). I swear when these beasts placed each hoof on the ground the surrounding houses trembled. It was just like in the film Jurassic Park, when the enormous foot of a T Rex drops on the ground with a heavy thud. They grew bigger and bigger as they approached and the photographer, whom I thought would be well used to this sort of thing by now, said "God they're the size of elephants". "You should worry," I replied, "You're not the one who's going to have to stand next to them".

I must explain that I've been a bit nervous of cattle ever since Rob, the dog and myself were chased by a herd of young steers, which are castrated bulls, just last year. We were walking through the fields near our home, the last one of which had this herd in it. Conscientiously, we put the dog on the lead and, with an insouciance borne of having done the same thing millions of times before, started to saunter through the pasture.

One of the larger, nearly fully grown steers took an interest in us almost from the word go and came over to eyeball us cautiously.

"Just press on," said Rob, unconcerned "He'll leave us alone in a minute",

At a slightly brisker pace we carried on walking into the middle of the large field, followed, at first, by the inquisitive bovine. The steer then darted round us and with slow head shaking started to bar our way. The thought crossed my mind that he may harbour some resentment against humans for having chopped off his two veg, but then I thought "No, don't be silly".

Now many farming friends have told us that cattle are very curious and just want to see what's going on and if they get too close just tap them gently on the nose with a stick and make a noise. It had been instilled in us that cows especially, are a nuisance, but essentially harmless, unless with their calves. Then you don't go near them at all. As this was a steer we reckoned it would be all right, but we didn't have a stick to hand, so Rob started waiving his arms and shouting a bit.

Instead of taking fright and running off, the steer responded by snorting and pawing the ground menacingly. Not the reaction we were hoping for. By this time, the rest of the herd, about 15 large, lumbering beasts, cottoning on to the fact that something interesting was happening, had crowded round behind the steer, effectively obstructing our way completely. Seen together the herd was monstrous, bellowing leviathans that could easily overpower us. Honestly, they looked like a bunch of fierce brown and white muggers.

"I think they're interested in the dog" Rob whispered.

We both looked down at her. She was crouching silently at my feet, conscious of the fact things were not quite right and attempting to sink invisibly into the ground.

"Just pick her up," Rob instructed, "Turn round and calmly walk back to the gate and I'll distract them".

I nodded "Ok. If you're sure."

So, lugging our heavy dog in my arms like a sack of spuds I began staggering as composed as possible across the field whilst in the background, I could hear Rob hollering and stamping the ground in an attempt to divert the herd's attention.

The next thing I hear is Rob screaming…. "OH GOD, RUN".

I panicked and in terror just legged it as fast as I could, without a single backward glance to see what was happening. But weighed down, I could only manage a berserk trot, the dog's head bobbing up and down, as I zigzagged across the field in a vain attempt to get away. It was only afterwards I remembered that you zigzag to avoid bullets not stampeding cattle. Ragged, laboured gasps escaped with each jolting step and, humiliatingly, also a little bit of wee.

I swear, as I tried to flee I could feel the heavy breath of that leading, deranged, ball-less bull on the back of my neck convincing me at any moment the dog and I would be mown down by the charging herd. I could see the gate in the distance, but no matter how hard I ran towards it, it never came closer. Sanctuary had never seemed so far away.

It was terrifying, running in slow motion, but how utterly, utterly relieved I was to reach the gate. The dog was thrown over the stile and I followed, practically vaulting the bars like a marine, seconds before Rob arrived with the entire herd close on his heels.

Viewed from the safety of the other side of the fence, the cattle, which were still bustling and nudging to get a good look at our dog, returned to the placid farmyard animals they actually are.

" If we ever tell anyone about this" said Rob, puffing and gasping and hanging onto the gate for support. "Then we'll have to say the cows had knives and machine guns."

Relating this tale in the pub later we learned the cattle were simply just interested in the dog. They weren't being aggressive or murderous, just intrigued. The dog has long black dreadlocks so I can understand their curiosity. Apparently what we should have done was let the dog go and made plenty of noise. The steers follow the dog and, because dogs can run faster than cows, our animal would have escaped and we could have passed through the field quite easily.

The experience has really shaken me up though and now I avoid walking in fields where there are cattle. Especially if I'm on my own. But like the true professional I am and for the sake of my brand new business, I stood nervously, with Rob, in between these two half-ton, white faced, Hereford bulls and had my picture taken, whilst I tried not to think about the fact they could squash me to a pulp without even noticing. Though, the adrenaline, causing my heart to pump faster, did make me forget how tired I was for a while.

13. The Chef   June 2006

Two weeks ago, I was full of hope and excitement. We had, sort of, bought a pub, and Rob and I intended to attract new restaurant customers by playing the perfect hosts with as much bonhomie and hearty friendliness as you get in a Butlins Holiday camp but with proper food that isn't smarty-pants posh or ping-ping (that is - bought-in, frozen microwave bilge). Is it beginning to work? I really don't know.

The restaurant is definitely holding it's own, but I wonder if most of the customers are flocking either because they enjoyed the food when the Ex-Landlord was running the place and have come back because they think it's still him doing the cooking or they are holidaymakers from out of town and have little or no other choice if they want a decent, reasonably-priced pub meal. Either way, I'm not complaining. We have a fairly buoyant restaurant trade throughout the week and are really busy at the weekends. Who cares if the success has nothing to do with us at the moment? Just as long as they keep on coming.

I'm pretty sure we are also seeing a greater number of customers in the bar or perhaps it's the same customers visiting us more often. Either way, there does seem to be a few more drinkers each night than there were before and I'm choosing to believe this really is down to us. Although, Rob and I agree, it takes a really long time to build a reputation, so we are doing it slowly, learning as we go along because it's not worth throwing all our 'crowd-pulling' ideas in to the pot at this stage. We still need to get to grips with the basics of actually how to run a pub first. But we're managing. Slowly, but surely, I like to think.

However, Chef is keen to completely throw away the old menu and start afresh. His enthusiasm is admirable, but we've had to rein him in a bit due to the fact it's only been a short time since we took over and we need to keep some sort of continuity on the food front by having a menu that reflects that of Ex-Landlord, because his food bought in a lot of trade. I'm extremely reluctant to mess with it at the moment, especially as the previous status quo worked. Besides, our Chef leans towards the gastro end of the market, which is definitely not what the repeat customers are used to here. People hate change and we can't afford to lose the diners we do have so I think we should make adjustments gradually.

More fundamentally, we haven't really cracked the problem of the timings in the restaurant. The session starts ok, but then it droops badly in the middle and people have to wait far longer than we think is appropriate – up to an hour for food on really busy nights. Explaining to Chef that a delay of this long will cost us customers falls on deaf ears. This is where Chef's inexperience shows as he reckons it takes a while to create good food and the customers will just have to wait. A laudable attitude if you're a celebrity chef with a restaurant in London doing 200 covers every night, not so good when you're a tin-pot chef in the arse-end of nowhere doing 20 covers a night, very slowly. Especially as the sort of food he is cooking at the moment is not that much different to the sort of stuff our customers can get easily and quickly elsewhere.

It's all about pleasing your customers and whilst we know ours are enjoying the food, they are definitely not happy about the wait. Our gut feeling is that people will try a new place twice – the first time as a novelty and the second time to see if they were right the first time. So, if they enjoyed themselves and all the correct boxes are ticked on their first and second visits, they will continue to use you, be less judgmental on subsequent visits and more patient if something does go wrong as it can do from time to time. If they have a middling experience the first time and some of the boxes are not ticked they'll come back one more time to see if it's improved and, if it doesn't, then you've lost them for what can be a very long time.

I've had people come in who said they'd tried another pub -Oh, it must be 10 years ago now - had a bad experience and haven't been back since, in spite of the fact it's probably changed hands several times over the years. This sounds alarming, I know, but I'm sure I've been guilty of the same, dismissive attitude myself in the past. Looking at it from the other side of the counter now, this approach is both nerve-wracking and soul destroying, as we've probably got two opportunities, tops, to ensure people return for subsequent visits.

In spite of the fact we've explained to Chef, numerous times, the importance of not making our diners wait too long for their meals, it doesn't seem to make any difference. We start out fine, but by about the 5th or 6th order the wait for food stretches and mayhem ensues. It's very stressful for me because it's my pub, it's me people are blaming and I have to keep going back out there to face them and say, "Your food won't be much longer now".

I'm sure it must be very stressful for Chef too. If you have a delay, orders back up and you have to move very fast to try to catch up, usually in a panic. So today we stopped expecting Chef to sort this problem out on his own and called a meeting.

"What specifically causes the hold up?" Rob enquired. We were all sitting round the fireplace in the bar, smoking and trying to be informal.

Chef didn't answer straight away, just scratched the back of his head and blinked several times as if he was trying to think of a reply.

"Actually", he said eventually "I need an extra pair of hands in the kitchen".

Rob and I couldn't have been more stunned if he'd said he needed a sex change.

At the moment we're doing an average of 20 covers in an evening. This is pathetic, but I figure it's better to serve 20 people well than make 40 people wait a long time and so far, we're not even serving the 20 well. I'm deliberately keeping the numbers down and sticking to the procedure we agreed in the first weekend we opened - of only booking in one table of 4 every 15 minutes (or two tables of 2 – do you see how it works?). Also, we've had requests for jobs coming out of our ears – school holidays approaching you see - so we've employed washer uppers for every night the restaurant is open. We've suggested Chef also uses them as runners to save his legs, fetching and carrying things from the stores and the enormous walk-in fridge, which is housed in the barn outside the kitchen.

"But you said you could cook for up to 40 people on your own" I said

"Not doing this menu, I can't" he replied

"I thought we already discussed this," said Rob, despairingly "I thought you understood we only had a certain budget available and there was no room for extra kitchen staff".

Chef just shrugged his shoulders and blinked vacantly.

After much discussion we decided the only solution was to re-work the menu to come up with dishes Chef believes he can do on his own, because we simply cannot afford to employ a Commis Chef (someone who will prep all the veg and do the dirty jobs). We've also agreed it would save time if there were no hot starters only cold ones. Ex-Landlord did loads more covers than we're doing; single-handed, so there must be a way of doing it.

We sent Chef away to think about it. I do hope the restaurant service improves because the food side is the real profit making area of the business and without more covers we're not going to be able to make the money we need. Struggling to get across to Chef the importance of just getting the basic service right means we've actively avoided talking to him about promotions, special food nights, adding value with things like taster dishes and 101 more ideas we have for boosting the food trade. And I can't help wondering if Chef's desire for a Commis has more to do with some unspoken, inflated opinion he has of himself rather than any real need. Perhaps, because he's now Head Chef, the little bleeder feels he shouldn't have to do the dirty jobs. Doesn't he realise it's all hands on deck?

I never, for one moment, expected these sorts of problems. I assumed our Chef would jump in with both feet, like Rob and myself, and just get cracking. The idea I had a couple of weeks ago, that all we needed to do was be warm and welcoming to our customers seems hopelessly naïve now. Honestly, the struggle with Chef is a real worry, yet something else to think about. But still, let's see if our little meeting works. Fingers crossed.

14. The Incident   June 2006

There are times when life comes along and slaps you in the face. Ordinarily, as I think I mentioned to you before, I need a short, sharp smack, to wake me up to the fact the rose covered path I'm following is perhaps, not the best one. But this time the whack was more of reminder that you should always expect the unexpected. Let me explain.

Rob and I were, once again, sitting by the bar fireplace this afternoon having one of our usual cigarette and chat combinations (well, Rob was smoking. I was tucking into a shepherd's pie sandwich) which seem to be a big feature of our lives at the moment and is practically the only quality time we have with each other (I don't count the conversations we have when I'm lying in the bath trying to relax and Rob is standing in the doorway, blathering on to me about nothing, because, mostly, I'm not listening.). We were, in fact, discussing next year's smoking ban and how our indoor smoking activity will have to cease. Heavens, even in our quality time together all we do is talk about work.

During this gripping exchange the room went dark as a large, 56-seater coach pulled up outside the pub, blocking out the light.

"Oh shit" said Rob "Are we expecting any visitors?"

I shook my head "Not that I know of"

Neither of us wanted to investigate further in case we drew attention to ourselves. From the relative comfort of our bar stools in front of the empty grate we could only see the wheels of the coach as our window was too low to see much higher, but craning our necks we could just glimpse movement inside the vehicle.

"It's probably nothing to do with us. They must've just stopped to look at a map or something," I said hopefully.

We heard a whoosh as the hydraulics opened the door of the coach, then a pause. We held our breaths, willing them to go away. No such luck. There was a tentative knock on the front door. Rob and I looked at each other and gave a deep sigh of exasperation.

"We could pretend we're out" he suggested

The reason for our displeasure was this sort of thing had happened once or twice a day ever since we moved in to the pub, 3 weeks ago. It seems, regardless of whether we're actually open or not, a pub is viewed as public property and at any time the masses believes it can knock on the door and ask to use the toilet or ask where a particular house is or ask what time the bus is due or ask what time the shop opens. Honestly, it drives you mad. I realise my adverse reaction is disproportionate to the occasion, but for god's sake, aren't we open enough hours already? Are we not allowed a few precious minutes to ourselves?

If we're downstairs and the intruder catches sight of either one of us then we're forced to answer because he or she never goes away and, every time, just stands there tapping on the window with increasing impatience. However, if I'm upstairs, out of view, then I just ignore them all. I figure, they have to understand, when the front door is closed the pub reverts to a private residence and you'd no sooner bang on the door of a stranger's house and ask to use the toilet than you would take a dump on his front lawn.

So, as I said, there was a knock on the front door and just as we attempt to slink away quietly, someone peered in through the bar window and caught us trying to hide.

Resigned, Rob sighed. "I'll go".

I settled back down on the bar stool to finish my shepherd's pie sandwich, listening to Rob reluctantly sliding open the bolts on the front door. The closed door at the bar entrance muffled any conversation so all I could hear was plenty of heated mumbling, followed by a muted exclamation of surprise. I did wonder, mildly, what the request was this time, but I really couldn't be arsed to move enough to investigate further so waited for Rob to slam the front door and return to tell me what it was all about. Which he didn't do.

Instead, after quite a while, he wandered back into the bar quite dazed, leaving the front door wide open, which was a bit dangerous because we'd also discovered in the last 21 days if you leave the front door open for longer than a minute someone comes in wanting a drink.

"Is everything alright?" I asked.

"You're not going to believe this. It's a bunch of old ladies, a WI from Ludlow or somewhere." he slowly shook his head in disbelief "They want to come in for a cup of tea".

"What? A cup of tea?"

Now that really was a liberty. We're a pub for God's sake not a coffee shop and we're NOT OPEN. Buggery bollocks. Can't they see we're closed? Jesus, Joseph and Mary. Are we to never have any time to our selves? The bloody, bloody cheek of it.

I was appalled and indignant at the presumptuousness of these little, old ladies, but rather than agree with me, as he usually did, Rob was vigorously shaking his head.

"No, No, you don't understand. They want to come in for a cup of tea whilst they wait for an ambulance."

"An ambulance?"

"Yes. One of them has just died".

I had hardly taken in this surprising news when about 30 or 40 poor ladies, filed quietly, and very subdued, into the pub. Rob and I swung in to action, directing them to the comfiest seats in the restaurant and setting about making vast quantities of strong, sweet tea. Moving amongst them, handing out teacups filled with the best restorative liquid known to man, I could hear them whispering to each other in reverent tones. "Poor Eileen, she just fell asleep and didn't wake up".... "She didn't look very well earlier I thought".... "How good it was she went at the end of the day and not at the beginning"... "At least she didn't miss her day out, she was so looking forward to it" and so on.

It turned out that Eileen, had died only 10 minutes or so before, between the church where they'd stopped for afternoon tea and our pub, a distance of some three or four miles.

"I hope there was nothing wrong with the sandwiches" said one of the old dears.

Now you can say what you like about little old ladies, but one thing you cannot deny is that they do have the full measure of death. At their stage in life, they are probably fully aware of its inevitability, so are unimpressed when it brushes past them and takes a victim. These old ladies had the full attributable resilience and, I kid you not, by the time they'd drunk the first of what turned out to be three or four cups of reviving tea, the level of noise in the room rose rapidly, as they collectively agreed what a shame it was about

Eileen and turned their attention to other matters. Very loudly.

The only person who remained shell-shocked was the poor old biddy who'd been sitting next to Eileen and had discovered she'd died.

So, whilst life smacked me full in the face and taught me a good lesson in not always assuming a knock on our front door will end up annoying me, I also learned, to erase the effects of a sudden, close but unrelated, death, a nice cup of tea is all you really need.

As the paramedics removed the body from the coach, the police arrived to take a statement from Eileen's travelling companion, so Rob sauntered across the road to where the coach driver was hiding out, to see if he wanted a cuppa. The driver was not happy.

"I'm 67" he told Rob "I'm far too old to be dealing with things like this after last year's heart bypass operation". Rob made sympathetic noises. "The same woman fell down the steps of the coach last year" the driver continued "and broke her leg".

"Well look at it this way," said Rob trying to console him "At least she won't be giving you any trouble next year

15. The Chef Part 2   July 2006

Another two weeks have gone by and things on the food front are getting worse. It started, oddly enough, with the fact Chef did go away and have a think and came up with some dishes he reckoned he could cook by himself, to replace, what he called, the more labour intensive ones on the existing menu.

"Great" I said, and meant it, in spite of the fact I am full of trepidation about changing the menu so radically at this early stage. It really is a big gamble with our livelihood.

To display the menu, we use slates hanging by butcher's hooks off a couple of chrome poles attached to the wall. It might sound odd, but it looks great, really "country", to overuse the word. Sadly, it wasn't an idea of Rob's or mine but of the Ex-Landlord, so I do have to give him a bit of credit for it. It is a much more novel and interesting way of displaying the meals we have on offer, better than a chalked blackboard or printed menus. The downside is that I have to write on each slate with a chalk pen, which doesn't wipe off very easily if I have to change the dish and because the surface is so rough, my writing often looks like that of a 5 year old. Or someone very, very drunk. Also the slates aren't very big, so when Chef gave me his new dishes I very quickly realised his descriptions were not going to fit on the space available.

"Pan fried fillet of haddock, cooked with dill and served on a bed of rocket and tomato salad with a dressing of white wine, olive oil and chives" is not going to fit on a slate measuring about two foot by one foot. Not unless I write it really small and have to then either spend all day reading the description out to our more myopic clientele or purchase a pair of those cheap, reading glasses off a stand in the chemist as a "special service at no extra charge" for our customers to use.

So, obviously I cut it down to "Fillet of haddock with dill on a rocket and tomato salad with white wine dressing". Still sounds good eh? Chef went mad and accused me of undermining his efforts and questioning his authority. I asked him what he expected me to do given his description was like trying to fit the Magna Carta on a postage stamp and he went off in a huff and hasn't really spoken to me since apart from in monosyllables. I could slap him, really I could.

Rob, wisely, has kept well out of it, or at least tried to. Because Chef's not talking to me, instead he's taken to bending Rob's ear at every opportunity -not about me having the audacity to alter his precious menu descriptions. Chef's not as stupid as all that, to complain to the husband about his wife - but instead, he's grumbling about the state of the kitchen.

Now we've listened to Chef pontificate at length about how can't possibly speed up when preparing meals, about the menu which is too difficult for him to achieve on his own, how he thinks the customers should just wait for "good food" for however long it takes to arrive, about the raft of extra help he needs. We've tried to resolve these issues with him and instead of meeting us halfway and at least being mature enough to accept some of the problems are his responsibility, he's now moaning about the state of the kitchen.

I'm actually astounded. We deal with one problem and think we've solved it and another one pops up to take its place, like pimples on the face of a teenager,

Now the kitchen, whilst tiny, is quite well equipped with a range oven, 6 gas hobs, a combi-oven (microwave/grill and oven combined which cooks very quickly), two deep fat fryers and a couple of catering microwaves plus a state of the art extraction system and enough pots, pans and utensils to sink a ship. Honestly, there's so much stuff in there it's actually quite difficult to fit the chef in.

Nonetheless, in accordance with Chef's latest wishes (demands?) and with the permission of Ex-Landlord, because the Pub's not ours yet, Rob has installed a hot plate and light, an electric warm-cupboard for crockery, new worktops, a fly zapper, mesh on all the windows and a fly screen on the back door. Rob has also removed the shelves from under the food serving counter and replaced them with an upright, chrome-finish pole to hold the worksurface up (for hygiene reasons, apparently) and the hot water boiler has been moved to allow more room to put dirty crockery prior to washing up. The kitchen is now beginning to look like a room Mike Robinson would be proud of. Which is an achievement believe me.

So, because the kitchen has been sorted a bit more to Chef's liking and because the menu has changed, plus all the starters are now cold dishes, I've upped the amount of covers I'm taking in the restaurant. Now we're doing an average of 30 on Friday and Saturday nights and 20 in the week. Not a huge amount, I know, but, thankfully, this level of diners actually means we do make some money.

After all Rob's hard work, however, the timings in the restaurant have only improved a little bit. Service still badly sags in the middle, especially on a Friday and Saturday night. I'm hopping mad really, but holding my tongue. The upside is at least we are doing more orders at the beginning of the session before it all goes array. And when it does go wrong, the wait has gone down to only about 45 minutes. Is Chef getting there? I really don't know.

I make sure I pass on to Chef when people sing his praises and I keep telling him, during service, that his food looks good and smells wonderful. So our previous frosty exchanges thaw and by the end of the session we're positively matey. But then, the next thing I ask causes him to be in a bad mood with me again. The other day, I suggested that when he comes up with a new dish, to write a cost sheet for each ingredient so we can see a) the total cost of each meal and b) what we are able to charge for it making sure it fits into our usual food offering and, crucially, still makes enough gross profit margin. I created a form on the computer and gave him several blank copies for him to use in the future.

I must admit he was a bit quiet when I handed the forms over, but I didn't really think anything of it. It was only when a scrap of paper came out of the kitchen with a brand new dish description, plus a price, on it for me to write on a slate, did I realise he was boycotting my cost sheets.

I tried not to storm into the kitchen to confront him, just sauntered in there waiving the piece of paper he'd left for me in the restaurant. I enquired, pleasantly, if he'd filled in a cost sheet and he said,

"No, I haven't".

"How did you arrive at this amount then?" I said calmly, pointing at the piece of paper in my hand.

"I have a gut feeling for the cost of things, so I added it up in my head and it came out with that price" Now he was pointing at the paper too.

"Oh. I see" What he really meant was – he'd guessed. I can't run a business based on guesswork. However, there was about 15 minutes to go before we opened for dinner. There was no way I could argue with him at this point, not only was it inappropriate, there was a good chance he'd stomp off in a temper and leave me unable to feed my diners. I was tempted to pick up one of the "special" Chef's knives we'd bought and stab him with it, but I couldn't see one in the immediate vicinity, so, instead, I just beat him to a pulp with a marrow I found on the work surface.

I can't take this level of stress. It's a little over a month in to our new venture. Both Rob and I have had the steepest learning curves of our lives. We are struggling to cope and every day we're bought down to earth with a bump because of some minor detail Chef wants us to sort out, which he lets us know about by mentioning it, to Rob mainly, about 53 times a day. He seems to be completely missing the point that he has to speed up the production of meals in order to completely satisfy our customers.

I sometimes wonder if we're just demanding too much. Perhaps all chefs are this temperamental and we want him to do far more than they are usually expected to do. I don't know. My experience of these things is minimal. I have worked with chefs before, but only when I'm just delivering the meals they have prepared. I know chefs can shout and swear a bit and get stressed out, but I thought that was just during service, which, in the restaurant trade, is quite acceptable. What I didn't expect is this sort of difficult behaviour could spill over into the quiet times too.

I can't find any information about how to run a catering kitchen either and I've trawled the Internet looking until my eyes and fingers bleed. I need to understand procedures and timings so we can suggest changes and help because it's blatantly clear that Chef is unable to solve these problems for himself. To put the tin lid on it all, just as we caved in to his 'suggestions' of how to improve the kitchen and finished all the work, he's now started bleating on about the number of hours he's working.

If it wasn't for the fact his food is good and I don't know if we'd just end up with someone worse, given we only had two to choose from in the first place, I'd kick his ass out of the door tomorrow. God, I'm exhausted.

16. The Drinkers   July 2006

It's becoming clear to me that one of the main assets of our pub is the folk who drink here. Of course, I hear you say, that's obvious - customers mean income, but I hadn't considered before that the drinkers are also, in fact a selling tool. It's probably hard to view Maurice as a sales executive when he's doing his party trick of balancing a full pint on his head, but we have come to realise that the people who choose to frequent our pub unconsciously attract other drinkers. It's not rocket science, this, but it hadn't really occurred to me before – people appear on spec, hoping to bump into someone they know, and hey presto – the next thing is that we have a busy bar with plenty of atmosphere.

The food trade is buoyant and there's no denying diners definitely bring in more profit, but they arrive, they eat and they leave, with a bit of banter along the way. The real socialising done in any country pub is with the drinkers. The ones that come in regularly and stay a while for a drink and laugh.

So we would like to make ours an eating AND drinking pub because there are precious few left nowadays. Too many owners are chasing the restaurant trade. I can see why, but in a pub like ours, which is, of necessity, a way of life rather than just a job or a business, only being a restaurant would be very boring, because diners come in and just talk to the folk on their table. They are extremely unlikely to wander over to another table, pull up a chair and join them for dinner. And they are even less likely to ask me to join them too. But all this happens with the drinkers in the bar, because it's a much more sociable pastime.

However, the problem is whilst people will come from far and wide to eat, there is no way they are going to travel for a drink. Drink-driving laws are strict and no-one wishes to contravene them. Being a pub out in the sticks means the only people who can get here without driving too far is the locals. So in order to create that all-important atmosphere for a pub, then we need to attract locals.

It's July now and we've spent a great deal of time trying to work out how to build the drinking side up from the barely alive it was when we arrived and I think we found the answer. It's two-fold, cultivate the cricket club and periodically give away free food.

The cricket ground is only out the back, so it makes sense for the players to drink in the pub itself, but over the last few years they haven't been doing that. So we set out to find out why, or at least Rob did. Cricket is deathly dull. I can't feign an interest even for the sake of my business. Can't work out how the scoring works. And what's all that about stopping for tea and sandwiches in the middle?

But that's by the by. It turns out the reason why the Cricket team has not been dropping in for a beer or two (or five or six) after a cricket match is because the Ex-Landlord was not overly welcoming. In fact he was positively frosty, I'm told.

I know none of the facts, so I can't tell you exactly what the problem was, but I have witnessed the Chairman of the Cricket Team, after four or five lagers, pushing his face into that of a fellow drinker and droning on and on unceasingly, about historical cricket scores and play tactics. The chairman usually corners someone by the bar and backs him or her into the wall from where there is no escape. The only thing this week's lucky recipient can do is cast beseeching looks over the Chairman's shoulder at other cricketers, who just laugh and walk away, never rescuing the poor individual in case they catch the attention of the Chairman themselves. So, I can understand really, why the Ex Landlord didn't encourage the cricket team to use his facilities, he was probably scared of being of trapped by the village equivalent of a British Rail Service announcer.

Nonetheless, Rob who professes to have no interest in sport whatsoever but somehow manages to understand all of it, even ice hockey, and who has a peculiarly effective way of escaping from the Chairman (Rob tells him to shut up and stop being boring– and the Chairman does, then never seems to take offence), first of all, took a long hard look at the alcohol on offer and made some changes (which seemed to involve adding more lager). Secondly, he approached the cricket club with the offer of sponsorship.

Instead of just giving money away, however, Rob proposed a deal whereby for every home game he would supply a barbeque and some food and the cricket team could sell burgers/sausages to each other, to supporters and the opposing team in order to make some money for the club. The cricket team whole-heartedly approved and has asked Rob to join their fund raising committee. Rob has already planned for them an Auction of Promises and a quiz at the pub. Way to go husband – what a star you are.

This simple effort and a bit of cash in the guise of barbeque food has reaped rewards no end, simply because our village cricket team appears to use cricket as an excuse for drinking. At every home game, and there seems to be one every other week, we now shift loads of lager and for away games the team meet in our pub before they go on elsewhere to their match and, more often than not, return to our pub for a drinking session afterwards. Saturday nights are becoming increasingly lively, what with the regular trade, plus the cricket team and their supporters. We just have to try and get the busy nights to spill over into the quieter weekday evenings now.

The second tactic, I mentioned earlier, to bring in punters, was the giving away of free food. Putting bowls of chips or sausages or roast potatoes or some such hot sustenance around the bar for customers to nibble on is a nice touch, especially as there are some people who will stay in the pub; until their last meal is a dim memory and they have grown so hungry their stomachs are touching their spines. But it's definitely a careful balancing act this one, because you have to bring out free food with just enough infrequency to make the customers grateful, but not so much they come to expect it. It's a difficult one.

I suppose a third tactic to increase the drinking trade, is the fact that Rob and I are determined to play the hosts. We both think this is very important. We want everyone to feel they are being welcomed into our home and made to feel comfortable and part of our little pseudo-community. So, once I've finished serving the diners, I always join Rob at the bar so we can take it in turns to mingle with whoever is in that night. As a marketing activity, it's not up there with 'Happy Hour' or a 'Shot of Vodka for a Quid', but it is something you don't often see in pubs - an identifiable host who's there to make sure you are well served with beer and having a good time, a bit of a Unique Selling Point I reckon. We also introduce people if they don't know each other and have this process off to a fine art,

"Oh hello, Jim, have you met Geoff? Geoff was just telling me he's got a ram with the same problem you had with one of yours What did you do about it?"

And they're off. You give them a few minutes, smile fondly and withdraw gracefully knowing it's a job well done. The next time either of these drinkers come in the pub and spot the person they've just been introduced to, they'll feel comfortable enough to chat and often, friends of either join in aswell and everyone just gets to know everyone else. It's lovely.

In fact, I stood behind the bar this Friday night and just surveyed the scene with a great deal of smug satisfaction. We'd been intermittently busy all night, but by about 10.30 or 10.45pm it had quietened down to a hard core of about 20 drinkers. Their ages ranged from early 20's to middle 60's and, I must admit they were all men, apart from Sarah, one of the part-time barmaids, and myself. But – and it was a big but – instead of gathering together in quiet cliques of two or three the whole 20 were in one big group, with Rob somewhere in the midst of it, all talking together and having a real laugh.

At one point another customer – I think it may have been a farmer, dirty, weary and thirsty from the last of the sheep shearing who'd popped in for a pint - was welcomed loudly and encouraged to join the throng. To me, it was incredibly heart warming and felt like a real achievement. All these people knew each other because they lived in the village or on the outskirts of it, but we'd provided them with a place to meet and chew the fat, to catch up on the gossip or to find out how the new Combine was performing. There was a real sense of community and I was honoured they felt comfortable and encouraged enough for it to be my pub they chose.

Of course we did the only thing we could, under the circumstances, Rob bought out some free chips and sausages for the customers to nibble. And I supplied the tomato ketchup and vinegar. A cheer went up when the food arrived. That really is gratitude for you.

17. The Long, Hot Summer   July 2006

A month and a half in and already I'm encountering the Great British Public in increasing numbers and whilst I'm happy about this, it does make me wonder if a few switch their brains off sometimes when they come in through the front door. I have recently been asked questions like:

"Oh, I fancied scampi and chips and it's not on the menu. I don't suppose you've got any in the kitchen have you?"

"Why yes" I reply, pleasantly "We have a stockpile of scampi outside. We just didn't bother telling you about it".

Or I've had one or two who look at the descriptions of all the appetizing dishes on the slate boards of which there are 8 starters and 8 main courses and say,

"Is that all? Don't you have a specials board?"

"Of course we do", I answer "But we don't advertise our specials board in order to give you the fun and pleasure of trying to guess what's on it".

One diner actually asked me the other day if the food was good. "No it's crap," I told him.

Sarcasm aside, I'm more than prepared to overlook minor exasperations like these because our business is blossoming. Perhaps the gloriously hot weather this year has something to do with it.

Summer is very kind to our Herefordshire landscape. The hedgerows are overgrown and untidy, which is just the way I love them and the fields shimmer with the flourishing wheat just before the monster Combines get to work. The calves are getting bigger and the sheep are newly shorn, which makes them look all white and new. At the moment, when you walk down a country lane in the middle of a week day afternoon, everyone is either at work or trying to cool down inside their houses, so the air is still, the heat creating a hush. It's lovely. The countryside around the pub is wonderful at any time of the year, but summer is always my favourite.

The only problem is that more people want to eat outside in our large beer garden and it's a long schlep from the kitchen to deliver their meals. Because of the extra walking, at the end of my shift I feel exhausted and, just when I was getting used to it, my legs once again feel dead and my feet hurt at the end of each day. I know, of course, it's only good business practice to allow customers to eat al fresco. I'm not complaining, honestly, just commenting, but why do the customers invariably sit as far away from the pub as possible? The garden is very large; so we've deliberately placed all the garden benches close to the pub to minimise the walking distance, but the diners, invariably drag them away to the furthest corner possible.

I'm also sure these outdoor customers are convinced I don't get enough exercise because, not only do they sit as far away from the kitchen as possible, they wait until I've made three or four journeys to deliver their food before asking if we've got any mayonnaise.

Yes, the problem with hot weather is it brings out a lot of people, which means plenty more opportunities for them to piss me off. One of my worst frustrations is the lack of urgency when diners book a table. An insouciant approach to eating out is understandable, because for the most part it is a leisure pursuit, but we do have a system for ensuring things run smoothly in the restaurant, so you don't have to wait ages for your food (or at least as short a time as Chef can manage). The crux of that system, the lynchpin on which the whole fragile construction rests is that you are not late for your booking.

Almost everyone is kind and considerate and turns up well before the time their table is booked. But you always get one or two who don't and it's those tardy types that really mess things up for us, especially if say, the booking is for a table of 8 and 6 people have turned up but not the final two. Obviously, all the on-time diners want to wait for the latecomers and this eats into the time we've allowed to cook the meals for the party. If a party is booked early in the evening and they don't order until well after the time allotted, then the rest of the evening can go horribly wrong. There are times when I have to organize the throughput of diners with the same military planning and tactical precision you would to invade a small country. It makes me want to tear my hair out.

So, latecomers annoy me, but conversely, so do those who are too eager or too impatient. My pet hate is at lunchtime when customers enter the pub on the dot of 12 – as soon as the doors open. I think it's rude somehow. I know that attitude is unreasonable because we do open for business after all. But at 12 o'clock I'm still putting the nozzles on the fonts (technical term for the beer taps), getting the menus out, putting the plug in the glass washer and a thousand other little jobs that all need to be done before I start serving. This should all be done before 12, that's obvious, but I never leave enough time to complete all the tasks, even if I rush, so, I'm always hoping the first customers don't appear till at least 12.10pm. I'm always affronted when they do but Rob says I'm just being perverse and should get up earlier.

However, on a Sunday it's different. The village has its own bowls team and each Sunday, the bowls team congregates outside the pub just before 12, waiting for me to open. Even 30 seconds late opening the door elicits complaints, but strangely I don't seem to mind. I'm convinced it's really important to impress this group of people. They are the stalwarts of the village, the oldies who've seen landlords come and go over the years and have seen a lot they can compare us to. And my competitive nature wants me to be the best.

Mind you, it's tough staying calm. Every week they all drink the same thing – a pint of Hancocks in a handled glass and I have to then pour 4 or 5 pints absolutely perfectly or else they'll complain about that too – oh and I have to remember which one drinks out of a straight glass. After two pints of Hancocks each they move on to scotch and, again, I have to remember who has ice and who doesn't and who has a splash of mixer and how much. It's like dealing with a bunch of unruly and demanding three year olds except, perhaps, these boys don't move about as much.

To distract them I've asked the chef to supply some free food each week, just the ends of that week's joint of beef, along with roast potatoes, Yorkshire pudding and a bit of gravy for dipping. We serve it to them all in one bowl and they fall on it like a pack of ravenous dogs. Even though one of them always complains the meat isn't rare enough, I think they all appreciate the gesture. The impatient way they jiggle their empty glasses on the bar, wordlessly insisting on another drink, tells me they do.

They're all getting on a bit, but one of the boys is in his eighties. I see him absent mindedly drive his car around the village sometimes and I always wonder why they let people so old on the road when their eyesight, hearing and reflexes are probably worn away. He takes about half an hour to reverse out of his parking space, revving the engine loudly but only moving a few inches at a time. Anyway, he's a dear old sole who pinched my bum the other day with a twinkle in his eye. The old rascal.

This is certainly a world apart from our lives before we entered the pub. Our days, then, were spent designing brochures, adverts and leaflets. I mainly worked 9 to 5 with the weekends off and I'd only leave the office for the occasional visit to clients to show them our latest winning design. The only pressure or stress I encountered then was when the photocopier chose to chew up my 14-page document.

Why we decided to take on the pub is anyone's guess. We really didn't think it through properly, I see now. I'd been watching 'Location, Location, Location' on the TV. Kirsty and Phil were trying to buy a pub for a mother and daughter and I'd thought. "Hmm, we could do that". Our local pub was up for sale at the time, and had been for a few months, with no obvious purchasers. So, Rob, who's as equally impulsive as me, said, "Let's have a look at the books first", and the rest, as you know, is history.

I think our main incentive for buying a pub was the immediacy of the income. By that I mean, with a graphic design and marketing company you have to spend weeks persuading the client you can do the work, then you have create the work, and then you have to spend a few more weeks trying to get payment out of them. With a pub, as soon as someone steps over the threshold, they've decided to spend money and they'll give you their cash before they leave. It's makes a refreshing change, I can tell you. Of course, there is the argument that you have to work harder to obtain a smaller amount of remuneration, but we'll gloss over that little fact.

I will also grudgingly admit that, whilst I can be a bit vocal about it (and it's only to you, believe me) the little exasperations, as a result of the foibles of our customers, are only a few. Mostly, I manage to hold back any sarcastic remarks (and my sarcasm has been learned at the feet of the Master – as I'm sure you are aware), so the Great British Public never experiences my aptitude for the lowest form of wit.

18. The Chef Part 3　　　　　　July 2006

To try and encourage things to run a bit more smoothly in the kitchen, Rob and I wrote a document for Chef entitled "Key Performance Targets."

The three of us usually have a weekly meeting to go over menus, any big bookings we've got coming up and to discuss any problems. It starts off calmly enough,

"We need to make sure meals are served quicker" says Rob, or something along these lines.

"I'm trying," replies Chef

"But we never seem to get anywhere and customers have to wait too long" Rob points out.

"It's not that long," says Chef

"I think 45 minutes is too long," says Rob

"Good food takes time," says Chef

And the meeting then degenerates into a slanging match. Chef and Rob scream and hurl insults at each other and I have to try and calm things down. It happens every time. The only uncertainty about the whole proceedings is not whether Rob and Chef will argue, but how long it will be before the shouting actually starts. So, because of all the loud noise, Rob thinks it's possible Chef isn't absorbing any of our wishes and directions and the solution is a written record of Key Performance Targets, which is, really, a list of goals for Chef to achieve.

The KPTs include aiming for a specific gross profit margin on food overall, by buying cleverly and costing food out on a spreadsheet before adding new items to the menu. Checking deliveries properly, signing off invoices, ensuring weekly records are kept for the EHO and, of course, those all important timings in which it is acceptable for the customer to wait for their meals. We've based this part on our own experience of dining out and on how long it takes for our minds to waiver from the conversation at the table to wondering where the hell our food has got to. We reckon the ideal is 15 minutes wait for a starter, allow 10 minutes for the customer to eat it and, then, once plates are cleared, their mains should arrive at the table within a couple of minutes. If no starter is ordered then a 25-minute wait for a main meal is tolerable.

It doesn't take a rocket scientist, or even a particularly clever chef, to work out from these timings how long he's got to prepare and cook food. But our chef received these instructions without agreeing to them, or even wanting to discuss them (Rob and I are not dictators, we do welcome input from him), which doesn't really bode well.

Nonetheless, as a sop to us laying down the law in this fashion, Rob said he'd help out in the kitchen on Friday nights, and has already done one shift. We thought this would not only appease Chef a little bit, but it also meant we could see at first hand exactly what is going on in order to suggest ways in which cooking times can be improved.

And an eye opening experience it has been, according to Rob. To start with, apparently, Chef is heating up soup slowly, on the stove in a pan. Now I know you think that's the proper way to do it but in a catering establishment such as ours it would be acceptable to heat the soup up quickly in the microwave. The soup, cooked by the chef, is homemade and tastes gorgeous. Microwaving doesn't detract from the taste or the quality. It makes no difference to the customer.

What it does mean though is there are less pans to wash up (because, at the moment, Chef uses a fresh pan for each soup order) and most importantly, it means soup can be ready in a very short space of time, and Chef doesn't have to keep an eye on it. Simple eh?

There are lots of other little ways that Rob has suggested Chef could cut corners in the kitchen, the most important one being, probably, that Chef should do more preparation beforehand – like cooking a few baguettes at the beginning of the dinner session rather than cooking each one as its needed due to the fact it takes up to 10 minutes to cook a baguette to accompany a bowl of soup. Or leaving the salad out of the fridge, because Chef knows he's going to need it again in the next 15 minutes, rather than keep putting it away. This is much more time-consuming than it sounds because the fridge is a large one, housed in a barn, across a courtyard. I dread to think how much time Chef could save by not fetching the salad and putting it back 500 times a day.

However, as you may have already guessed, the Key Performance Targets didn't work. Timings of the food haven't improved and Chef has not implemented any of the suggestions Rob put forward.

I really can't understand it. Nothing we attempt seems to work. We'd be better off trying to persuade a plank of wood to serve meals faster. We have completely run out of ideas of how to resolve this situation. So, as we are now entirely at the end of our tethers, and in a last ditch attempt to sort this out, we decided to speak to a consultant, someone who'd both run his own pub and been a chef.

The consultant visited us a few days ago. He made sympathetic noises as the problem was explained, in depth, and then went away to cogitate and compile a preliminary report about his thoughts on the matter, which arrived in the post today.

The Consultant seemed to really grasp where we were coming from and his report was very supportive of us – He'd guessed of our extreme fatigue and discerned we were only half way up a steep learning curve and, hence, were inexperienced with all things kitchen. He also said that we shouldn't worry if we can't overcome the problems with the chef -we can just replace him. My god he made it sound so easy. For a moment there a little light came on in my mind and I could actually see the end of the tunnel.

In a nutshell the Consultant reckons that, understandably, Chef probably lied about his experience to get this Head Chef's role. He reckons Chef has the required culinary skill, but is lacking in sympathy and understanding for our operation as a whole and given that he actually worked in the kitchen alongside Ex-Landlord for a few sessions before accepting the job, should not be moaning about the kitchen and his hours six weeks later. The Consultant also reckons Chef does not have any hands-on experience in several of the areas we find him lacking, but would have probably embellished what little experience he did have to protect his pride and to also land this job.

The Consultant also believes that Chef's aspirations are completely different from ours. Whilst we are trying to achieve a proper country pub serving superb, home cooked food, Chef is after accolades, stars and rosettes. Apparently, by using the word "control" in the job description we have given Chef the impression he has total power over his culinary kingdom and that Chef needs to learn that he has responsibility, yes, but that, ultimate control lies with Rob and myself.

The Consultant did tell us off for probably making the Chef feel 'got at', what with our KPT document and all. Apparently, it's not that the Chef doesn't deserve it rather some of things are beyond his experience and, this is causing Chef concern, which is manifesting itself constant demands and moans.

I must say, it all seems very obvious when you put it down in black and white like that, I can understand that we've come across a bit heavy, but both Rob and I have been bought up in work environments where written targets and expectations are the norm and it never occurred to us by this simple action we were just making things worse.

As I've mentioned before, Chef is not very old and, obviously, it is now clear, very inexperienced. We were expecting him to embrace a role that is evidently out of his depth and we are unable to teach him because Rob and I don't know what we're doing either. There are no short courses, books or even articles on the Internet that can help. Believe me, I've looked.

We've decided the way forward is for the Consultant to have a private chat with Chef to get his personal view of the situation and to ascertain what he is capable of and to what extent he needs help, so we've scheduled a meeting for the end of the week.

I'm not convinced this is going to work, but I do feel a lot happier about the situation. Perhaps it will all end happily. I certainly hope so, because we've spent £400 on the consultant already. What with all the "improvements" we've made to the kitchen as well, this bloody chef is costing us a fortune. I think I will write some KPT's for myself, the first one being – do not spend any more money on the chef.

19. The Regulars　　　　　　July 2006

For a bit of light relief from the problems in the kitchen, I was standing behind the bar the other day listening to the absolutely inconsequential conversations my customers were having in the pub. There was that odd mix of ages and trades you find in small community pubs such as ours. One group was some youngsters off the estate up the road, who all meet for a quick drink after work and are still here three hours later.

A couple of drinkers had particularly dirty jobs and were still in their work clothes, looking grimy and sweaty, but no one minds that at all. This is what a public bar is for. Workers and farmers like a pint and as their jobs can keep them busy well into the evening, we want them to come in without feeling they have to dress up or indeed take off their muddy boots. The floor is tiled, so it's easy enough to sweep the next day.

Another group consisted of a chicken farmer in his sixties who also breeds welsh cobbs, one cattle farmer in his early 50's, one sheep, arable and equestrian livery farmer in his middle thirties, an electrician in his late 30's, who comes from farming stock and still farms occasionally and a digger driver, also in his late 30's. They were talking about a new tractor one of them had purchased and went on to compare farm machinery in general and, whilst their conversation to me was quite boring, to them it was as significant and opinion forming as if they were discussing religion or politics.

These guys are completely individual whilst, at the same time, representative of rural living as a whole.

Or at least rural living round here where everyone, it seems, is self-employed.

When I first met Maurice, I asked him if he too was a farmer since he lived on a farm at the top of the hill above the village.

"No" he said, "I dig holes".

"Oh do you? With a shovel?"

"No" He rolled his eyes and almost, but not quite, tutted. "With a digger" He plainly thought I was stupid so, starting again, I established that he too was self employed and had a digger, which he rented out along with himself as operator.

"Are you very busy?" I asked, somewhat surprised, never having thought you could have a whole career, or indeed a reliable source of income, from creating holes in the ground

"Oh yes" he replied 'People always needs holes".

"What for?" I had visions of Maurice being paid to remove earth randomly from around people's property, much in the same way you'd pay someone to set off fireworks - for fun rather than for any real purpose.

"Drainage, sewage, ponds. Lots of things, even swimming pools"

I'd clearly underestimated the importance of his hole-digging service and wandered what other jobs I'd missed that were providing livings for men with machinery.

Maurice is an extremely large, slab of a man. Very tall, at least 6'4" and sturdy, with powerful arms, a ruddy smiling face and an extremely sunny disposition. Every time he comes in the pub he's smiling and laughing and always has a particularly amusing turn of phrase.

One day I overheard him talking to the electrician who was bemoaning the fact that, as he was about to become a father again soon he would be unable to have sex with his wife for a few weeks (this is the sort of conversation you have to get used to in the bar of a working man's pub). Maurice nodded sympathetically, then offering encouragement said,

"There is one way you can keep having it away"

Puzzled, the electrician asked how and Maurice replied

"Just hope the baby comes out the sunroof"

One of our most amazing customers is Edgar who, at 86 doesn't look a day over 65 and is as sprightly as a 40 year old. Edgar whispered to Rob and I once that he was in the Navy as a youngster and had stormed the beaches at Normandy on D-Day. Once the words had left his mouth Edgar squirmed in embarrassment as if he'd just belched in polite company

Another favourite of mine is Harold. In his early sixties, Harold has farmed in the area all his life and married a farmer's daughter. I've seen a wedding photograph when he was in his late 20's. Harold had been very handsome and wouldn't have looked out of place in Sinatra's rat pack. Now he is heavy, with a florid, weather beaten face and wisps of short, white hair waft across his head, but he still moves with the lithe grace of a fit man and his stockiness and well built shoulders hint at the fine figure he once was, in spite of the fact he's grown one of those hard, round beer bellies that are the ever present badge of a man of a certain age.

Harold always appears irascible, but perhaps it's just his face that looks grumpy because he's never very argumentative or sullen, although every time I see him in the pub and ask how he is, Harold always replies "terrible'. I thought he was taking the piss, until someone told me recently Harold is a diabetic and some days can be quite ill as the diabetes takes control.

Harold, unlike any of the other customers, never spreads gossip or tells anything he knows. And boy does he know a lot. He's grown up with practically everyone around here so he certainly has the sources at his fingertips. All he does if the others are commenting on what someone is up to is nod and say "aye", but never imparts what he knows. I said to him once,

"You never gossip do you Harold" and he answered proudly "No, never".

He likes his beer though and it's really hard to see how many he's had, as they never seem to have any effect. The only time I'd seen Harold seriously drunk was when he'd been drinking all day at a funeral. And the only way I could tell was he smiled and laughed a bit more than usual. Harold is not supposed to drink much because of the diabetes, so when he first came in to the pub and asked for a pint of diet coke, I was supposed to know, somehow, that he didn't really mean it and to pour him a pint of Hancocks instead. He took great pleasure in scolding me about that one believe me

This is a ritual now that occurs every single time Harold comes in to the pub. He asks for a pint of diet coke then gets loudly peevish when I pour him one. Mostly I ignore him along with his gripes about the beer (no-one else complains and we certainly shift a lot of it), his moans at having to wait longer than a nano-second to get served and his protest at only getting half a pint at the end of the evening, in spite of the fact that's what he's asked for.

In a very short time Harold has become part of the fabric of my life and there have been a couple of times when he's popped in for a pint at lunchtime, we've had really decent conversations about the state of farming. As you find a lot in these cases he is an extremely intelligent, talkative and knowledgeable person underneath that gruff exterior.

Most of the time Harold pops in at lunchtime and stays a while, but once he flew in and demanded a pint of cider – quickly. I said,

"What's the rush Harold?"

"I'm busy aren't I – hedge trimming" and sure enough, parked outside the pub, was a flail hedge trimmer used to cut hedgerows. The vehicle was so large it was blocking out the light. Its engine was still running and it chugged away blowing little puffs of smoke out its exhaust pipe and making an incredibly loud noise.

"Oh, I see", I replied, understanding his urgency.

Harold had parked the farming equivalent of an armoured tank outside the pub and left the keys in the ignition. "You'd better hurry then"

"Oh I think I've got time for just one more," says Harold with a grin, waggling his empty glass in front of me.

Yes, the regulars are the lifeblood of our pub. Without them we would surely sink and I cherish each and every one of them. It's my life's work to try to make them happy even when, in their own sweet way, they vaguely frustrate me. I was having a conversation with one of them the other day and he was trying to explain to me where his house was.

"You go up the road, the one opposite the pub, and go as far as Billy Watson's place."

"Billy Watson? I don't think I know him. Does he come in the pub?"

"No. He's been dead for about 20 years now."
"So how will I know which is his house?"
"Oh you can't miss it. It's the one right by where the old 'phone box used to be."
See what I mean?

20. The Chef Part 4   August 2006

Well the consultant had his meeting with Chef and we received the report a few days ago.

Basically, consultant was right when he said Chef felt 'got at' and that Chef thinks our approach is demanding and overbearing. Chef feels we don't understand how difficult it is running a commercial kitchen and, rather than our suggestions for change helping, we are in fact hindering the process. Chef wants try running a whole business rather than just part of it. He'd really have something to moan about then, I can tell you.

I'm not going to go into any more detail because, frankly, every extra sentence I write makes me want to punch Chef in the face even more and I realise this is not the most calm and reasonable approach from an employer. Enough to record that I think what Chef has to say indicates what an inflated sense of his own importance he has. It seems he thinks we owe him a job and that he's got us over a barrel because we will sink without him. That's what you think matey.

I wanted to sack Chef on the spot, but Rob, being less reactionary than me, said "No. Let's deal with the issues and see if we can resolve this situation once and for all". So Rob has spent his time off today talking to the Chef about re-doing the working areas of the kitchen, putting up shelves and cupboards so we can remove all the "storage items' that aren't used that often, like blenders, away from the working areas and ensuring that everything the Chef needs during service is as close to hand as possible to minimise any faffing around. I'm not quite sure how, in his head, Chef rationalises the removing of all the cooking equipment from the kitchen with producing meals faster, but I've let that one slide by. It's not going to help matters if I point it out, is it?

I'm afraid we've also relented on the Commis Chef, mainly because business is improving all the time, so we think it's probably a good idea to employ one. I know Rob helps the Chef on Friday nights, but he can't devote any more time to it, and anyway, Rob's more than needed to play host in the bar, so an extra pair of hands a few more nights of the week would be useful. Happily, there's a lad, called Rory, who lives down the road, who's training to be a chef and is interested in a job, so we've left that up to Chef to ask Rory if he's willing to come and work for us. Rory's already done one shift as a 'try out' so we know he's more than capable and willing to learn. Just to put in our two pennyworth and to not let Chef think he's having it all his own way, we've insisted he serves larger portions of vegetables with meals, because we think this would add value without really increasing the cost too much.

So far, we've spent close to £700 we haven't budgeted for trying to sort this problem out, what with the Consultant fees, new shelving and stuff for the kitchen. Given that we've tried our hardest to please the little bugger, I hope Chef appreciates it.

I'm sure you've experienced this and I'm not sure if it's a trait peculiar to just men or, indeed, to employees in general, but some people really do think they are the only ones capable of doing their jobs. They seem convinced that if you do make the big mistake of letting them go, you'll realise how indispensable they are and, like a regretful ex lover, be on the phone day and night begging them to come back and save you?

Perhaps, it's arrogance, ego, and a complete lack of humility or just human nature. I don't know, but I've seen so many examples of an over-developed, but misplaced sense of self-regard when I had a proper job that I've lost count. And, sadly, in my experience, it's usually men that are guilty of inflated egos, not women.

Not all men, of course, just ones who have reached a sort of middle-management status. Perhaps their bravado and self centredness is actually a clever disguise and what they're really trying to convey is they're scared shitless of losing their jobs and really don't know what they're doing. But instead of acknowledging these weaknesses and being the better man for it they're going to pretend everything's ok by acting like complete knobs. Either that, or the power has just gone to their heads. And when they rise further up the corporate ladder, it just gets worse. In the past, three men have propositioned me at work; all of whom, coincidentally (or not, as the case may be), were Managing Directors of the companies I worked for.

I suspect these men were on power trips and wouldn't believe for a moment, given their positions of control not just over the company, but also over me, that I could fail to fancy them. Obviously, I said no, because, honestly, in each case, you could punch clay prettier. I had my standards to think of. And besides, I was convinced if the worst came to the worst I could always get another job. Hard to believe now I was so sanguine about it, especially in this day and age when some women sue if a male co-worker so much as looks at them sideways.

I'm rambling I know, but this brief foray into how much I despise people (men?) who think they're the bees knees, is just an excuse to put off telling you that, despite having tried to make his life even easier than it was before, inevitably the chef predicament is not improving. We did not manage the situation once and for all as Rob had hoped. In fact things are getting really bad.

It really would be fine if I thought Chef was at least trying to improve his output, and there'd be a little more regard for him if he had a bit of humility and listened to what we had to say, instead of insisting he knows better. Although, there is a chance on this point I'm wrong – It's just assumption on my part that Chef spends his days thinking he knows better than either Rob or myself, because, frankly, Chef never actually says anything apart from to moan that he hasn't got enough shelving or enough workspace. When we all have a meeting Chef just sits there, looking blank and obviously not listening and then, when we've finished, just goes off and carries on doing whatever it was he was doing before. Perhaps we could beat the information into him with a big stick.

Today, Rob asked Chef if he'd managed to get in touch with Rory, the local lad we've got lined up for the Commis Chef job. It was decided Rory would be useful on Tuesday, Wednesday, Thursday and Saturday evenings and on Sunday lunchtimes. Chef was tasked with contacting Rory and offering him the job. After Chef told us that he'd lost Rory's number and we found it for him again, we just left him to get on with it. So, this morning we asked what the outcome was.

Chef told us he's managed to get in touch with Rory, but that Rory wouldn't be available until 10th September and then could only do Tuesday evenings. This seems a little odd; Rory never mentioned before that he was unavailable for work for six weeks or so. It's now the middle of August, so Rob asked Chef what he proposed to do about it given the fact we'd agreed he could have some help in the kitchen. Chef mumbled something about putting an advert in the paper or contacting the catering colleges, both of which he expected Rob to do.

Rob said no, that it was Chef's responsibility to find his own assistant and to go away and write a job description and come up with a plan as to how he was going to find someone to help.

We had a very slovenly session this evening, in spite of the fact we only did 14 covers. I'm presuming this is because Chef is thoroughly demoralised. We've been banging on for weeks about not making people wait too long for their meals, but this evening all the customers had to wait an age and when the veg went out they had about 3 carrots and a sprig of broccoli each. Not good in Herefordshire where loads is the standard.

I realise, by now, you probably think we've spent the last couple of months browbeating our chef until he's become a little blob of unresponsive jelly. You may think we've been bullies and poor Chef can't cope with the pressure we've been putting him under. You may be right. But we have a fledgling business to nurture and all we ask of Chef is to understand that what we see as important is what he should see is important too.

In the end, in desperation, Rob, himself, went round to Rory's house and, thankfully, Rory's willing to work the sessions we'd hoped for and able to start straight away. In fact, Rory's first shift is this Thursday evening. Now how difficult was that? If the Consultant thinks, as employers we've been 'overbearing' and 'difficult', he wants to try working with our Chef and see how long it takes before he shoves Chef's head in a pan of soup.

21. The Complaint August 2006

Last week, on an unusually quiet night, I spent an hour chatting to a customer about Tarmac. I say 'chatting to', but in the main he droned on at me. Apparently, the stuff we use in Herefordshire isn't a patch on the Tarmac in the Isle of Wight and the island's sleeping policemen are impressively constructed mounds of tar and aggregate. I learnt this at the beginning whilst I was actually listening. He probably went on to explain why our tarmac is inferior, and why our sleeping policemen earn his contempt, and why they are better in the Isle of Wight than the rest of the country, but by that time I was running through a mental list of all the things I had to do the next day and trying to decide if it would be bad to have a fish finger sandwich before bed. That's the thing about being a landlady. You don't half meet some boring people.

We have this sort of unwritten rule if someone is in the pub on their own then we have to talk to them. We have to stay to keep those customers company even if they're so dreary you want to chew your leg off. I hope I've perfected an expression that says, "I'm so fascinated by everything you have to say" whilst I am in fact thinking about something else entirely. Rob doesn't have the patience to talk to the regularly tedious ones for very long and always makes some excuse to be off doing something else – probably poking his eyes out with a sharp stick or watching grass grow – but me, I just think it's my job to stay and take the worst they can throw at me.

In the past few weeks I've not listened my way through conversations about, accountancy, plasma screen TV's, cricket, football, and the exact dimensions of all the rooms in someone's house. There are probably loads more dull subjects I've failed to mention, but I wasn't paying any attention.

To be honest there are only one or two really uninteresting customers, but what amazes me is why these offenders don't know how tedious they are. How can they fail to see the glazed expressions in people's eyes and the lack of any response apart from "yuh" or "no"? How do they convince themselves that what they saying is so absorbing it doesn't require a response? What can possibly be the point of that man telling me the room dimensions in his house? Was he simply showing off? Which, by the way, was entirely wasted on me because I was completely unable to envisage whether the sizes he was relating translated to large rooms or small ones. Or was it his way of trying to pull (hard to conceive of, I know)? The man was wearing a wedding ring so; perhaps this strange method of wooing had worked in the past. You can imagine the conversation when he met his future wife,

"Now my bathroom measures 9ft by 10ft, but that means my third bedroom is only 7ft by 7ft".

"Really?"

"Yes, but my living room measures 14ft by 9ft and my kitchen is 8ft wide by 19ft long"

Perhaps then, when her eyes rolled back in her head and she fell into a coma, all this man had to do was tip her over and drag her off to the nearest church or registry office.

Customers can be quite strange or some, like all of us, at least have peculiar idiosyncrasies that seem to manifest themselves most particularly in my bar. What we don't get, though and contrary to what you'd expect, is much insight into their psyches. It's not often people tell me their problems or pour their hearts out to me and for their reticence I'm truly grateful.

Although, one customer did have a moan the other day. He told me his neighbour has 15 dogs all of which bark in the early hours of the morning and then intermittently throughout the day. He said the dogs would bark at even a leaf falling from a tree. Apparently, they're positively rabid with excitement when the postman arrives. The neighbour's dogs set his own 3 dogs off as well so, with 18 dogs barking all at the same time, the area where he lived had the noise levels of a small municipal zoo. All the folk living in the neighbourhood, about 6 houses worth were upset and outraged at the continual disturbances.

I asked my customer if he'd complained to his offending neighbour and he said not yet, but if the noise goes on any longer then he'll be forced to.

"How long have you had to put up with this?" I enquired.

"Eleven years" he replied.

So this unfortunate customer was prepared to moan about the problem, but not actually do anything about it. As a nation we certainly like to grumble don't we? Have you ever been on holiday abroad in the vicinity of other British people? They'll be the ones griping that the taverna down the road doesn't do full English breakfasts or they can't get a decent cup of tea or the shop doesn't sell proper biscuits, like custard creams. Makes you wonder why they bother going abroad at all doesn't it?

People moan, but moaning is a world of difference from your actual complaining. Moaning is just another name for whingeing, which is just a whiney and irritating noise. However, in most trades that deal with the public, a complaint in itself can be quite a constructive exchange of information. If anyone has a complaint and they bring it to our attention then we can do something about it and send the customer away happy and satisfied that we've at best dealt with it or at worst noted a problem. But not to complain, to just go away and moan or whinge about it to as many people who'll listen I think that's quite evil and insidious and sadly, I've been guilty of that very thing myself in the past.

Now I'm in the position where customers are the lifeblood of my business, I positively welcome complaints (you know what I mean). I want to know if there's something wrong with the food or the beer. I want to know if the restaurant is too warm or too cold. I want to know if there's a draft or the ladies' toilets smell funny. If I know, I can put it right, but if you don't tell us we could be blithely offending customers and wondering why they don't come back. We're not losing business, I hasten to add, but you do worry. If there's something wrong I wonder if anyone will actually have the balls to inform us.

Sometimes it's hard to tell whether a customer is actually complaining or just moaning. Take the incident not so long ago. I served a table of four - three gentlemen and a woman - with mains, which they enjoyed, bringing out four portions of the bread and butter pudding with custard they'd ordered for dessert (made with panattone bread - delicious). The pudding was light and fluffy, cut in a square tower and wobbling gently as I put it down in front of them. I turned away to clear a nearby table, fully confident they'd be appreciating their pudding very soon, when a loud, piercing, voice rang out behind me,

"This is not bread and butter pudding. Take it away".

Startled, I turned back to the table of four where the voice was coming from. The woman's face was twisted in disgust as she eyed her untouched dessert suspiciously. She kept repeating, with a great deal of contempt "This is not bread and butter pudding, THIS IS NOT BREAD AND BUTTER PUDDING", in an increasingly strident voice that was beginning to catch the attention of all the other diners. I had to shut her up quickly, so I asked her, as nicely as possible, what the problem was,

Again she said, "This is not bread and butter pudding".

At the risk of infuriating this customer further by pointing out the obvious I replied,

"Er...it is bread and butter pudding. It's made with bread and butter in the same way as usual"

"Well it doesn't look like bread and butter pudding to me. Take it away, I don't want it". I asked her if I could get her something else, and she just rudely shook her head and waved me away in a dismissive manner whilst her three other dining companions tucked into their puddings with gusto.

I picked up her pudding plate and took it back into the kitchen, quite astounded. This woman had made no attempt whatsoever to taste her dessert, had no idea that it was very good, flavoursome and comforting and was, in fact, much better than your usual, run of the mill bread and butter pudding. Silly cow.

Now was that a complaint or a moan? I told you sometimes, it's hard to tell. I would say it was a moan, but the customer would definitely think it's a complaint. We had failed to ensure our bread and butter pudding lived up to some unknown benchmark in her head. If it is a complaint, how do we put it right for her? It's impossible to deal with.

I did the only thing I could do in the circumstances, a coping method tried and tested on the one or two boring customers that frequent the bar. I ignored her, whilst looking like I wasn't.

22. The Winning Idea   September 2006

Given my background it's tempting to bang on about the power of marketing, to pontificate how, as a pub, you must have a differentiation, some little gimmick that sets you apart from the crowd, a hook that pulls the punters in. But I really can't be bothered to think about it. What with learning to run the pub, dealing with Chef and forgetting to eat, I'm much too weary.

I'm also more than a little worried about where our winter restaurant trade is going to come from. It's the beginning of September now and we must be getting pretty close to the end of the season. The summer has been full of tourists so how are we going to make any money when they go home?

Our pub is tired, the menu is all over the place, the food takes an age to be served, our bar is searingly bright and lacking in atmosphere and, worst of all, your hosts for the evening look half dead and in need of a hot meal. Knowing all that and the fact you are going to share your bar space with several large spiders painted into the woodwork, would you come in for a meal? Probably not. Thankfully the tourists have been, but they'll all be going home soon.

Rob and I have tried to look at the big picture, to come up with winning marketing strategies that will promote our business far and wide, but we're too tired. The most I can plan at the moment is whether to have cheese and onion or salt and vinegar crisps for tea. I'm a disgrace to my former profession and a sickeningly perfect example of not practicing what I preach. My former clients would be appalled. Good job most of them don't know where I am.

We serve food and drink, surely that's enough? If I open the door the customers will come flocking, won't they? Of course they won't. Why do you suppose so many pubs have regular karaoke nights, Sky Sports on the TV, theme nights, quiz nights, live music, happy hours, pool tables - it's all designed to attract punters, because the drink alone just isn't enough anymore.

The only problem is that more and more pubs use the same activities to draw in customers, thus negating the uniqueness. If all pubs around where you live have Sky Sports they are no different to each other. How then do you decide which one to visit? You probably end up at the one closest to home so you don't have to drive. Am I right? I am.

Rob thinks we should have topless barmaids. I think the lack of food is making him light headed. If I were topless behind the bar then the locals would just think I was a bloke with lipstick on. It really wouldn't help.

I don't think Sky Sports, karaoke or even me with my non-existent tits out would attract the locals who live round here. They're more the Radio 4, Daily Telegraph sort of people, which means our pub is probably not posh enough for them. I've told you before it's a bit spit and sawdust (and that's just the old blokes in the bar). We really do have to decorate, assuming of course, we ever get to buy this bleeding place.

So what are we going to do to attract the locals in the winter? How are we going to persuade the villagers to leave their warm and cosy cottages on dark and damp winter nights, with a pocket full of cash they can give to us in exchange for beer and food? I've said before one of the main assets a pub has is the folk who use it. The locals who frequent our pub at the moment do not seem to mind that the decor is shit or the stools are hard to sit on or the light burns your retinas. I do not kid myself, however, this is because of the compelling hosts behind the bar or the delicious beer we serve. Oh no, the reason is simply one of habit, because a regular once told me he used to frequent this very same pub years ago when he first moved to the village. The pub was so bad then they only had a few customers (including the guy relating the tale), so they never used to buy much in the way of actual kegs of beer. Instead, if a thirsty patron popped in they'd send someone off to the local supermarket to buy a few cans.

Nonetheless these ardent stalwarts, who have been drinking in this pub for years, through thin and thin, are, slowly but surely, attracting other people, people who are keen to pop in for a pint and a chat. As a consequence, at least once a week, our bar is actually quite busy, especially as, at this time of year, the village and surrounding area plays host to a small influx of hop-pickers from Wales (or more likely these days from overseas). And because of the cricket team our pub is also busy at the weekends too. For the bar side at least it's a start. So we must make sure we keep happy those who frequent our pub at present and they'll bring in other drinkers. I don't pretend for a moment it's the best marketing strategy in the world, but it's a plan. Of sorts.

The problem really is the restaurant, where all the trade, currently, is from out of town. Food is the biggest earner; it provides the profit and has the biggest spend per head. Without the food trade we would be dead in the water, our swollen and grey backsides pointing heavenwards. For drink alone is barely worth dragging myself out of bed for at 11 in the morning, but the food side is where you can make some serious money. It's also where most of the problems lie, as I'm sure you are more than well aware.

There's no getting away from the fact we have to improve our culinary offer, and here I don't necessarily mean the food. No, I think that the moment diners walk in through the door they should be feasting with their eyes, the surroundings should reflect the level of the prices they are expected to pay. You can get away with a restaurant that looks dilapidated and tired if all you are providing is something with chips for £2.50. Our food is well cooked and all that, but possibly, I hate to say, verging on the gastro. Whilst we don't charge a huge amount for it, we charge more than we can seriously justify due to the surroundings and the interminable wait for the meals themselves. Luckily our present customers are largely holidaymakers from down south who think our food (and beer actually) is quite cheap compared to the staggeringly large amounts they usually have to pay for sustenance at home.

Of course the simple answer is to change the type of food we serve, making it cheaper and less fussy, but how on earth are we going to get the chef to do that? He can't grasp the simple fact that all our worlds should revolve around the customer and not around him. Our inexperienced chef has not the faintest comprehension that keeping our customers happy is paramount.

The simpler dishes we have persuaded him to cook still fall into the chef's "slow food, not fast food" ideology. By this I mean that the chef's own working philosophy, completely unsupported by or even agreed with Rob and myself, is that good food takes a while to prepare. This is fine as a concept in itself and works extremely well for places such as The Merchant House in Ludlow, an award winning restaurant, but cannot in no way be used when the sort of stuff you're selling is steak and mushroom pie with chips, albeit all homemade with, so-called, hand cut chips. No, even with a bit of chopped parsley sprinkled on the top this dish is only one or two steps away from the sort of thing Fray Bentos creates. And you can't make diners wait for up to three quarters of an hour for that and expect to get away with it.

Nonetheless, the idea of a concept is a good one. You only have to read A.A.Gill or Giles Coren, the restaurant critics in the Sunday and Saturday Times to understand there are plenty of 'concepts' out there to be tried out. Especially in London, where there are so many restaurants it must be really difficult to make yours stand out from the crowd.

The independent small restaurants in London embrace fine dining but still all hang it around a concept. One has gone for the 'country in the city' idea with dried hops on the ceiling and a menu that reflects all the traditional main dishes - fish and chips, sausage and mash, belly pork, that you normally get in proper, 'real McCoy' country pubs. The only difference is that in the London city, fake, country-pub your beer-battered sustainable pollock, with a Jenga-like pile of square cut chips, will set you back the price of a small semi-detached cottage in Herefordshire. You get the idea. Only, if you do venture out to experience the real countryside and the pubs therein, they're all doing the same 'country' theme. Hence, there's no differentiation, nothing to choose between them and, as a result, most are just ticking over, trade wise. So, the irony is, if you wish to be a roaringly, successful country pub - you need to be in the city.

Other London restaurant 'concepts' include cooking on a Hibachi Grill at your table, New York style Italian tapas, sushi on a conveyor belt and only mussels on the menu with expensive imported beer.

Now look, I said at the beginning I couldn't be arsed to bang on about differentiation and I've gone and done just that. I've berated you with marketing science, the little I know of it anyway and I do apologise. Perhaps my lapse is a cathartic attempt to purge my frustration? A futile quest to try and make sense of it all and see a bit more wood than tree. A serious attempt to share my worries and, thus, seek some sort of inspiration. It hasn't helped though because. I've not managed to come up with any award winning ideas.

Hang on though. Just wait a goddamn minute. We do have a concept, I've just realised. We've got a performing monkey in the kitchen.

23. The Chef Part 5   September 2006

Today was momentous and extremely frightening – we sacked the chef.

In a move that will probably herald the end of my business, my hopes and dreams and, most definitely, my cash, we took the unexpected step of asking him to leave. Surprisingly it was me who had to give him the bad news and, annoyingly, he didn't turn up for the lunchtime shift until 11.40pm. 20 minutes before we were due to open. This in itself is more than enough illustration that Chef has been taking the piss. You can't get ready to serve, who knows how many diners, in just 20 minutes. I took the coward's way out, though, and informed him of our decision at the end of his shift, rather than at the beginning. No Chef to do the cooking this evening, though.

Brave or foolhardy, I don't know, but Chef really has pushed us too far. There really are only so many tantrums I can take before I break. On the other hand - I've never been so scared of anything in my life before.

The previous night, Rob and I talked at length about what we were going to do to solve this Chef dilemma. Difficulties still occur on a daily basis, in fact, it's invariably the same problems day after day. Usually to do with something the Chef's not happy about in the kitchen. It's so wearing. In the three and a bit months since we took over the pub we haven't planned a single marketing activity or event simply because all our time has been spent sorting out or worrying about, or arguing with the Chef.

At the beginning of what now seems like an inadvisable adventure, I pictured myself as hostess of the most warm and inviting establishment this side of the Malvern Hills. I would welcome customers with a smile and a bit of banter. I'd offer them an array of interesting real ales, alcoholic beverages and enticing food. I'd be the mistress of my little empire and people would leave happy and satisfied having enjoyed a hearty meal, congenial company and the warm appreciation of an oak beamed Tudor building. Nothing sophisticated of course, but an authentic, country-pub-experience the like of which is fast disappearing. But it's not really like that.

On closer inspection the beautiful, beamed building is falling apart, the décor is exhausted and cluttered with enough mismatched knick knacks to resemble a flea market and some of the equipment, like the glass washer in the bar, is on its last legs. We know naff all about running a catering kitchen and are worn out with the Chef difficulties and the weight of the paperwork. Understanding the accounts, employment tax, national insurance and VAT is like trying to decipher the mysteries of the universe and explain them to my dog. Smiling heartily at customers is actually quite difficult when what you really want to do is sob.

It does seem running a pub is not that easy or at least Rob and I are not finding it a walk in the park. In order to keep costs down we only employ a tiny handful of part time staff, (except Chef) so, most of the jobs we do ourselves. This is making us tired and irritable.

The responsibilities are divided between the two of us so that, in the main, Rob looks after the bar, which involves a lengthy, and time-consuming sequence of procedures, all designed to make sure the beer tastes good, the bar is clean and tidy and we never run out of anything.

So most days Rob's breaching, then settling, or tapping the three real ales we keep, ordering or taking delivery of stock, checking or mending equipment, emptying bins, going to the wholesalers, washing beer towels, cleaning shelves, plus a million and one other things that needs doing around the pub like mowing the lawn or fixing the guttering. He's also been sorting out the kitchen for the Chef of course.

This is apart from serving customers for a few hours, making them feel welcome and supporting me whilst I worry myself sick about everything Frankly I think the man deserves a medal. Based on having no experience whatsoever, Rob's doing a grand job, if the feedback is anything to go by.

Me? I just waitress in the restaurant, do the accounts, fire staff (it appears) and float about trying to make people feel welcome.

Owning and running a pub is one of the most time consuming, trying, debilitating, claustrophobic and downright frustrating situations I've ever been in. But the bit that keeps you going, the one thing that really drives you on day after day is that we're determined not to let it beat us. We want to make it work and are absolutely committed to building an extremely successful business.

Running a pub is not all bad, of course, only about 80% of the day, and there are times when it can be quite satisfying and the odd occasion when it's quite fun and our regular customers contribute most to that. Even the boring farts, to some degree, are endearing. I feel grateful to these villagers who've taken us at face value and have made us feel at home. And it didn't take that much free beer either. Perhaps they actually understand what we're struggling to achieve. Struggling, being the operative word.

So, we are Chef-less and this formed the crux of what Rob and I discussed last night. How are we going to cook the food? Remember we only had two replies last time we advertised and look how they both turned out. The first obstacle is finding another chef and the second is dealing with him or her once employed. Will we end up experiencing the same problems but with a different face?

It is a major league conundrum and one that needs to be solved quickly as we want Chef to leave straight away and we'll only close for food until the day after tomorrow.

So we talked and talked. And the outcome?

"I think I may have a solution," said Rob after nearly two hours of trying to look at the problem from all angles,

"Oh yes and what's that?" I replied, "Get the customers to cook their own food, but still charge the same amount?"

"No. My solution's better than that".

"Oh really? Just serve cold food then?"

"No, No, be sensible"

"I am being sensible. There's no real solution, which is what's stopped us sacking the chef before"

"I told you. I have a solution"

"And that is…?"

"I'll do the cooking"

"Wha…?"

Yes. It's hard to believe isn't it? But Rob reckons that working in the kitchen with Chef every Friday evening for the past few weeks has given him an insight into, not only how to cook our entire menu, but also how to prepare and serve it.

Now apart from the obvious benefit of saving us £20,000 a year plus bonuses, we will have full control of our kitchen. We will be able to create the sort of food we'd planned. We will be able to keep a close eye on the costs, we can put proper systems and procedures in place and everyone, including us, will be happy and satisfied.

I am keeping upbeat and trying to focus on the benefits here in order to completely ignore the fact we must be stark, staring, raving mad. Have you ever worked in a catering kitchen? It's very close to hell on earth. It's one of the most stressful and emotionally charged jobs you can do, beaten only by Air Steward on a crashing jet. I think the only thing I would be capable of doing under the trying circumstances of being a chef is panic. I'd have a complete nervous breakdown. Rob, whilst trying not to lose it altogether, will have to remain calm and composed, (which, I have to add, is something most chefs don't manage) cook different meals for one table that need to be all ready at the same time. And then do it again for an even bigger table. And make the meals look appetising. And, obviously, the food has to taste superb. And he'll have to keep up this level of quality day in and day out. Without poisoning anyone.

This is going to put the greatest pressure on Rob he's ever experienced. Working with me for the best part of the last 10 years will be nothing compared to this. You can see why, as I mentioned at the beginning, this is momentous and extremely frightening. So, Rob thinks he's capable of being the chef does he? I do hope he's bloody right.

24. The Kitchen   September 2006

So, yesterday, subsequent to Chef's departure, we stood together, Rob and I, in the kitchen, looking at all the equipment. My husband was gently quivering with barely concealed eagerness to get started, whilst I was quaking with fear and trepidation. The restaurant is closed for a couple of days due to 'kitchen refurbishment', so we do have a little time for Rob to settle in.

I must say, I have always admired my husband's ability to be able to concoct tasty and nourishing meals from all the left over bits and pieces in the cupboard. Rob can take half a can of tuna and a packet of cornflakes and create something good enough to be served at a dinner party.

I like to think I'm no slouch in the kitchen either, but I find the only way I can produce anything even remotely successful is to slavishly follow a recipe, never deviating from a set list of ingredients and a method. Even then the result can best be described as just nice, rather than simply delicious. Often, when I cook, I can place all ingredients for a stew in a pot - garlic, onions, carrots, prime stewing steak, a sprig of thyme and so on, and it comes out tasting a bit like a stock cube melted in hot water. Identifying any of the items that make up the dish is nigh on impossible. These are not my finest moments, I admit, and whilst sometimes it works, most of the time my cooking is the culinary equivalent of playing with plasticine in that you can mix together all manner and range of interesting colours – and it ends up just brown.

Rob, I think, is quite a culinary genius and can do things to gravy a wife can only dream about. You see, he is greatly more curious than I and thinks nothing of wantonly throwing in a bit of sage, rosemary or other herb we happen to have lying about. I view this casual approach to creating meals with deep suspicion. I'm as adverse to adding ingredients that do not appear in the recipe as I am to throwing fireworks on a fire to 'see what would happen'. The crucial difference between Rob and I, however, is that his inquisitiveness produces some truly memorable food and my slavish obedience just produces food.

I do trust Rob, of course I do. I know he'll be fine cooking the food in our pub. I have eaten so many of his meals I'm more than confident he can produce the tasty level of food we require. But you can't help worrying can you? As I'm hoping you've realised by now, cooking is only one part of the equation. The more difficult task is ensuring the meals actually leave the kitchen hot and on time in order that your customers are willing to give you money in exchange.

Nonetheless, I left Rob lining up all his utensils and cooing lovingly over the hand blender whilst I stepped through the back door outside into the fresh air to take deep and, hopefully, calming breaths.

I sat down on one of the chairs we'd put out there for the kitchen staff and, feeling a little better, lit up a cigarette. In the courtyard between the kitchen and the barn that houses the walk-in fridge and the dry store, I noticed the cracked paving had been blasted with a power washer and thought, 'Chef's been busy', and wandered over to have a look. Most of the floor was almost black with wet weather and a constant stream of dirty boots, but a small portion was pristine, like newly laid concrete. I was pleased Chef had made the effort before he left and looked around, trying to gauge how long it would take to clean the rest. What I saw then made me realise it doesn't take a rocket scientist to work out our ex-Chef was not a happy bunny. Scored into the dirty floor with the high-pressure water jet were the words "Pay rise".

'Hmm," I thought. "He had some hope". But, perversely, this made me feel a bit more optimistic. Seeing those words on the paved floor I remembered how bad it had all been. With Chef now gone a whole weight of strife, conflict and stress has been lifted from my shoulders and that's ignoring the fact more strife, conflict and stress may descend. No, I am choosing to believe that whilst I worry enormously about the effect Rob in the kitchen may have on our business, at least there is now hope and an end to the hostility and trouble that existed before. I am looking forward now.

"I think I'm going to need some practice first", said Rob sticking his head out of the back door.

"What sort?" I enquired

"Tennis practice. What do you think?"

I sighed. "I guess you mean cooking, but you already know how to cook"

"Ah yes, I know how to cook, but I reckon it would be useful to try preparing meals for people who've ordered at different times. A dining room situation. A restaurant work-out".

"Righto. I'll go and drum up some people to invite round for dinner whilst you check what we've got in the way of food, but first", I pointed to the floor, "Come and have a look at this".

Puzzled Rob moved over to where I was standing and glanced down to where I was pointing. At Chef's departing words. He read them carefully and his only comment was "Arse" and then he sauntered off to the walk-in fridge, humming under his breath and looking for all the world as if he was enjoying himself.

A few hours later five of our friends, plus my son and his girlfriend, were sat around a table awaiting food. I was the waitress, taking orders for 2 diners at a time, from a menu of 5 or 6 dishes and staggering the checks into the kitchen, just like a normal restaurant situation.

Having already taken the first order, two steak and mushroom pies with chips, I was waiting for 10 minutes or so to pass before taking the second order, which would be for three meals. I was on tenterhooks and daren't enter the kitchen in case Rob was in meltdown, although I wasn't sure whether it was better to stay in the restaurant out of the way or go in the kitchen and offer to help.

I waited until I'd actually taken the second order, one lamb shank on a bed of mash potato with port and sage gravy, one beer-batter fish and chips and one Mediterranean Chicken before poking my head, tentatively, round the kitchen door.

I found Rob wiping the rims of two big bowls full of steaming hot steak and mushroom pie topped off with gorgeously golden pastry.

"Piece of piss", said Rob throwing on some chopped parsley with a flourish. "These pies are ready to go. Come back for the chips and veg".

"Ok." I said uncertainly, "Er, I didn't realise it'd be that easy".

"It's easy because everything's been cooked beforehand", Rob explained. "It's just a matter of reheating the food and arranging it nicely on a plate".

"But it's only been 10 minutes and the first meals are done. We've never served a main meal in 10 minutes before, not even when you were helping out in the kitchen".

"Ah well, I have learned a few things, but couldn't put them into practice before. And besides, Chef was a bit of an arse and felt he had something to prove".

"I suppose you're right. Well the next order will test you a bit", I placed the check on the grab rail above Rob's head, scooped up the heavy bowls of steak and mushroom pie, whacked the kitchen door with my bum to open it and presented the dishes to our waiting guests.

A little later, when everyone had gone, Rob and I were having our habitual fag in the public bar in front of the fireplace and debriefing on the practice run. I commented he'd coped well and that everyone really enjoyed the food. It was hot and tasty and no one had to wait longer than 20 minutes for his or her meals to arrive. A successful exercise, I told him.

"Hmm" said Rob, doubtfully. "It went ok today, but this wasn't even the start of it. I hadn't actually made any of the food, so tomorrow I'm going to have to get in that kitchen early and start prepping. It's a lot of work. And", he added sadly, "I didn't try cooking any steaks today".

"Steaks aren't difficult. Are they?"

"Steaks are the worst".

"Why? It's just a piece of meat".

"Yes, a piece of meat that must be cooked in one of many ways – rare, medium rare, well done and so on. Getting them bang on each time will be a nightmare".

"Oh you'll be fine", I said, trying to sound supportive, fully confident that, after today's little session, Rob was capable of handling anything.

He took a deep drag on his cigarette and didn't speak, just stared into the empty grate for a moment or

two, whilst I stared at him anxiously. Eventually he stirred and said simply,
"Hmm, I do hope you're right".
Uh-oh. Rob sounds worried.

25. The Bar   September 2006

It didn't occur to me until sometime after I had actually agreed to it that, whilst there are many upsides to Rob taking over cooking duties in the kitchen, the one definite downside is that it's now up to me to run the bar. A more daunting prospect than it first appears because it's not just a matter of pulling pints, I have to ensure the beer is in tip-top condition at all times.

Rob says this is none negotiable as a pub that keeps bad beer is a pub with no customers, so not only do I have to learn to keep the ale & lagers well, I also have to be passionate and obsessed about them too. Otherwise the locals will complain quite vociferously if their drink does not, even in the slightest way, meet their exacting standards.

I do accept our customers are the experts as I never touch the beer myself and it's much better they complain loudly than leave quietly to drink elsewhere, so I'm more than happy to listen to them. But they are never as polite as I would be in this situation. And a few, core people do seem to carp on, long and often at the moment.

Over the past two weeks, since I took over the bar, one group of two or three locals has moaned, most unhelpfully, that the Hancocks doesn't "taste right" or "The ale's giving me the stomach ache" or "The beer's much better up the Swan" and one singularly brief "Yak".

As you can see, it's really hard to understand exactly what these regulars think is wrong. Obvious problems usually, are real ales that are cloudy or smell bad, lager that is flat or alternatively, too frothy, or Guinness that tastes too bitter. These concerns can usually be solved in one of three ways, either there's something wrong with the gas system that pumps the beer up from the cellar or the beer lines themselves are not properly clean or the real ale has not settled properly. We have the beer lines cleaned professionally and that has got rid of about 95% of the problems, especially with the pumps and the lines and I settle the real ales for as long as I've been told to by Rob (he's the one been on a Cellar Management Course, after all), so I'm usually fairly confident I can fix anything else. I also, have no complaints whatsoever from any of our other customers.

Though, trying to clarify exactly what these regulars think is wrong, only brings forth the same comments, so mystified and muddled I run up and down the cellar steps several times, getting all hot and sweaty. I check sell by dates, the beer lines and the levels of beer in the cask and emerge none the wiser.

This is the point at which I see the smirks and the sly grins and I realise the buggers are pulling my leg. All this group wanted to see were my bits jiggling as I ran frantically to and from the cellar. My anxiety has been their entertainment and in appreciation they usually offer to buy me a drink. Later, when I trap each of them individually after one of these incidents, and interrogate them to see what they really think of the beer, they usually manage a begrudging "It's alright", which, truly, is about as much praise as I'm going to get. The fact they spend hours drinking the stuff leads me to believe it's not altogether bad.

However, the other day one of my other customers, who is not known for any tendency toward leg-pulling said to me,

"This lager tastes really funny".

Now I'd noticed it was pouring a bit flat, but put that down to using glasses that were too warm and made a mental note to ensure they were stone cold before I pulled the next one. On the other hand, the frothyness or otherwise of the lager should not affect the taste.

"I changed the barrel at the end of the last night, yours is the first pint out today, perhaps that's what it is, the lager's sat in the pipes all night" I offered.

My customer picked up his pint and took another swig, grimacing as he swallowed,

"No there's definitely something wrong. It tastes bloody awful."

So off I went down the cellar to, once again, check the sell by date, the beer line and the levels. And do you know what I'd found? I'd mistakenly tapped the wrong barrel. The poor guy was drinking cider instead of lager. The cider was coming out of the lager tap. No wonder the lager tasted strange.

This is funny as I write it now, but I was annoyed at the time because I had to flush out the lager line with water until it was clean again and that took quite a while I can tell you.

So, as you can see, it takes a while to learn something as unfamiliar as beer keeping and there are still some fundamental things I've yet to overcome, like changing the gas cylinders. A beer cellar is not a woman friendly place, simply because everything is too darn heavy to lift or screwed on too tight to undo (the screw nozzle of a gas cylinder is a case in point. You need a spanner to do it and I just don't have the upper body strength). It frustrates me that there are some things this woman simply cannot do, so I resort to bribery to get the younger customers to lift the cask ale barrels for me. A pint for a barrel is a fair exchange and it seems to be working so far.

I'm trying really hard to learn the bar quickly and I think I have a shaky grip on what's required. Already I've done stock taking and re-ordering from the PubCo and I now know how long to settle the casks of real ale before the beer is ready to serve. It's not rocket science I know and many people have done it before me very well and I'm learning from the mistakes I make. Thankfully, I haven't poisoned anyone yet and I actually think, whilst I'm not quite there yet, it won't be too long before I'll be at that stage where I could, quite cheerfully, organise a piss-up in a brewery.

The one moment of uncertainty came when I had to decide whether to employ a bar person or a waitress. Because Rob is now in the kitchen it means there's no one to serve behind the bar if I'm busy tending to diners. So, despite the fact sacking Chef will save us a great deal of money, we've had to spend a little bit on employing a few more part-time staff to help when we are open for food. But do I get them to look after the customers in the bar or the ones in the restaurant?

I've plumped for letting them serve drinks because I figure it takes a lot longer to learn to serve diners well. But that means until at least 9.30pm there are no hosts to welcome in the drinkers. Oh God, I think my head's going to explode with all the new learning and the new conundrums I'm trying to stuff in it. It's a good job your brain doesn't get full up and in order to take on board something new you forget another vital piece of information. Can you imagine what it'd be like if the moment I learned how to tap a barrel, I forgot how to walk?

It's a very steep learning curve to running this pub. So steep in fact both Rob and I need crampons and a pick just to climb a few feet. Both of us have been cast into roles we never, in a million years, expected we'd have to grasp, he as Chef and me as bar manager.

I'm of the opinion that Rob is taking care of diners well, although the strain he's under is huge and our down time is an object lesson in emotional support. He's crippled with self-doubt and his frustrations and uncertainties are constant. Rob is extremely good at preparing and cooking meals, but no amount of telling him persuades him otherwise. Nothing at all seems to boost his confidence and the situation is not helped by the fact, we're also holding our breaths at the moment, watching to see if Rob's cooking is having a detrimental effect on our business. I'm pleased to report there has been no downturn in trade as of yet, but you never know, do you?

Even so, I have to massage Rob's ego at every turn, in spite of the overwhelming evidence he's doing a good job. We've had a very good summer, people are flocking and the compliments are pouring in left, right and centre and none of this seems to be dwindling. All I can do is hope and pray as the weeks go by, that Rob begins to believe he really can be the Chef.

To be honest, I don't think Rob is necessarily the weakest link here. My grasp on things is quite loose and I'm not in control as much as I should be. Don't tell Rob, but I forgot to shut the front door at the end of yesterday's evening session. The pub has been completely wide open all night. I couldn't have been more helpful to the thieves and burglars if I'd loaded our stock and the till into the truck and taken it to their houses myself.

In a minor panic I had a quick scoot round to check, but nothing appeared to be missing. How lucky was that? Either my unconscious invitation had gone unnoticed or the local criminals have taken pity on someone who is thick enough to leave the front door of a pub gaping open, throughout the small, dark hours. My growing ability to run the bar may be unquestionable, but if I'm going to forget even the simplest of tasks, such as locking up at night, then that makes me something of a liability, surely? I really must try harder. Obviously, I haven't mentioned it to Rob, not being in that much of a rush to let everyone know what a pathetic idiot I am.

26. The Smoking Shelter   September 2006

I've decided to shift the focus of my worry to something else for a change. Now, I'm a little bit worried about our smoking shelter. Or, to be more precise, the fact we don't have one. We are supposed to build one because, sometime next year we'll have to stop smoking in pubs. The Government has decided to implement a ban on the grounds of the dangers of passive smoking. Their aim is protect, not so much the customers, but the workers who have to spend a number of hours breathing in other people's smoke. As a smoker myself I'm not as adverse to this piece of legislation as you might think simply because clearing up at the end of the night, when a bunch of smokers have puffed their way through the best part of a packet of fags each, is quite an unpleasant task. I'm really only thinking of myself here, of course.

We have one customer in particular, who sits on a stool at the bar with a lit cigar. The more inebriated he gets the more expansive he becomes and so, gesticulating wildly, showers everyone in a 3ft radius with ash. I've taken to following the end of his cigar with an empty ashtray in a pointed attempt to catch the debris, but I'm wasting my time.

Not only does he not take the hint, he often brushes my clothes with the lit end, so now I look like I've been in an explosion, because I smell of smoke, am covered in ash and have burn holes in my clothes. Rob once handed this particular customer an ashtray and said, "That's for you to use when the floor's full." What with having to constantly empty full ashtrays, sweep stray fag ends of the floor and wince at the burn holes that appear in the furniture, I positively welcome the ban.

I don't know if it's a country trait or one peculiar to men of a certain age, but we do have a lot of smokers who frequent the pub. At the moment they are allowed to smoke in the public bar and at the top part of the restaurant, the bit near the bar, but if and when the pub is finally ours we intend to make the restaurant a non-smoking room completely –even before the ban comes into effect.

So obviously, with a lot of smokers we have a lot of customers who are not overly enthusiastic about the ban. They really are not happy. The smokers see it as interference in their civil liberties and I can see their point. I do explain, however, that the prohibition is not about subjugation but protection for the staff who have to work in smoky environments, but it doesn't console them. I think I'll just keep it to myself that I'm actually looking forward to it.

A lot of pubs will be affected though, particularly the land-locked town centre ones where there is nowhere for them to build an outside smoking shelter. We're lucky to have plenty of outside space and, being the only pub in the village, I can't see a smoking ban being more than a nuisance to our regulars. It certainly won't prevent them from coming to the pub altogether.

It's been reported in the trade press that we'll actually see an increase in people visiting the pub because those who hate smoke will be able to drop by. That's the official line anyway, but I don't believe it. The ban is already in place in Scotland and pubs experienced a downturn in trade of at least 10% in the weeks following its introduction. I really hope a drop in sales doesn't happen here.

It's now September and the Government has failed to issue us with any guidelines as to what our smoking shelter should be like. Unbelievably, neither has it decided on the date the smoking ban will come into effect. You just can't help thinking they really haven't thought this one through, can you?

I've heard the regulations will not be published until just before Christmas and the commencement date could be as early as April next year. This doesn't really give us much time to build a shelter or, indeed, save up the money for it. Until we are told categorically what to do, it is dangerous and potentially expensive; for us to plan or build anything in case it's wrong. The rumours are that it will have to be an enclosure with open sides. But is that none, one, two, three or four open sides? Will it have to be an umbrella or can we build an outside smoking room? I'm assuming we'll need to build something that can be heated and sheltered from the weather, but that's going to cost the bloody earth.

I intimated to one young smoker the other day that we had our smoking solution all sorted out, but that he might not like it – I told him that I plan to hand out plastic rain hats. Like the ones old ladies wear. He looked horrified

There's a good chance the smoking ban will come in before the pub is actually ours because, incredibly, we are still waiting to exchange and complete. It's the middle of September now and we appear to be no further forward than we were on the 1st June.

If you remember the PubCo had failed to gain permission from their landlord (the owner of the building) for Rob and I to take over the lease. That was a little over 3 months ago and still there's no sign of this permission coming through. I honestly cannot imagine what the delay is. No-one, including the PubCo itself, seems to know why it's taking so long, especially as it usually only takes a couple of weeks for this consent to be granted.

It's futile even trying to speak to any solicitor apart from our own. They refuse to take our calls. The only release we have for all the pent up emotion and frustration is to shout every day at the PubCo and this has bought quite astounding results, not the one we're actually hoping for, but other, entirely pleasing effects.

Just recently, the PubCo agreed to replace the dying glass washer in the bar with one that was bigger, better and, best of all, free and in August we received a case of 1litre bottles of vodka, which is a lot of vodka. If this sale doesn't go through then at least we can get drunk and wash every glass in between shots.

As the delay has dragged into September, Rob has excelled himself. He was on the phone to the PubCo today accusing the staff of being less than professional, telling them the hold-up is losing us a lot of money (not sure how he works that one out, but there you are) and that if completion doesn't happen within the next week, then we're walking and will be going to the press to spill the beans about what a complete and utter waste of time it is having a pub with this company. Now those are threats.

Rob went on to add that he wanted to know what the PubCo was going to do to really compensate us for all this stress and the fact we still didn't own the lease to this pub and that he wanted someone, who can make an actual decision to phone us back today with an answer. I'm so glad my husband is in my tent pissing out, rather than out there pissing in.

At around 4 0'clock this afternoon we received a shamefaced call from a PubCo boss, who offered us two free barrels of ale, lager or cider – our choice. This amounts to a piffling £200 or thereabouts. So, knowing he had the biggest leverage he's ever likely to have again with the PubCo, Rob told them it wasn't enough.

"What do you want?" said the PubCo Boss nervously and Rob's reply can only be described as an object lesson in genius-level blagging, a real example of what you can get if you really have the cheek to ask.

"I want you to pay for a smoking shelter in the garden."

When I heard this I stared at him in shock. We'd never discussed compensation on this scale. Admittedly Rob hadn't decided exactly what he was going to ask for, he was going to test the water first to see what he could possibly get away with, but I just thought it'd be a few weeks supply of beer or a bit knocked off the rent. I never imagined he intended to go for broke.

There was a tumbleweed silence at the end of the phone, then the PubCo boss stuttered and stammered, probably as astounded as me, but gathered himself together enough to say that he was unsure what type of smoking shelters will be necessary but would go away and find out before promising to ring back very soon with an answer.

Indeed, half an hour later, the PubCo boss was back on the phone. He hummed and ha-ed a bit more and said we will need a structure that is at least open on 1 side, possibly with a roof and heating and if we agree to allow the refurbished area to be used as a "showcase" to other landlords, he would consent. Ah, the man from the PubCo, he said Yes!

Rob did a thumb's up sign to me and I started jumping up and down and clapping my hands together in excitement, just like a small child, but my exerts were brought to a sharp halt when I heard Rob say,

"I've been thinking and realised it's no good having a nice smoking shelter to show off when the courtyard area it'll be in is incredibly untidy and needs sorting out too. Will you do that as well?

I think by this time the PubCo boss had come to the conclusion there was no point in holding out, so, remarkably, he said yes to that too and agreed to send someone over in the next week to have a look at what was required.

All this amounts to thousands and thousands of pounds worth of work. I'm still flabbergasted and Rob can't believe, either, the spectacular outcome of his outrageous demands. Once Rob had finished on the telephone the pair of us clasped arms and danced around the bar together in glee.

27. The New Regime   September 2006

So, moving from the smoking shelter in the garden to the catering facilities, let me warn you that what I'm about to write is a tortured analogy, but it does best illustrate a Saturday night in our kitchen.

When I was a kid I used to sit and watch TV in the evening with my mum and dad. Saturday night viewing centred around a programme called "Opportunity Knocks" which, essentially, was a talent contest, much like today's "Britain's got Talent". This show was responsible for launching the careers of many a luminary such as Freddie Starr, Spike Milligan and Les Dawson. It also gave us the visual delights of a bloke who won six weeks in a row by flexing his stomach muscles to the tune of "Wheels Cha Cha" and another who's act consisted of bashing himself over the head with a tin tea-tray whilst singing "Mule Train".

Another sophisticated turn was a chap who balanced twirling plates on spinning sticks. The object was to keep all the plates gyrating for as long as possible, by twizzling each rod if the plate started to slow down. To ensure the crockery never fell, thus negating the point of his act, the man had to run around in a frenzy, dodging backwards and forwards between the sticks, tweaking this one, adjusting that one and winding up another as if he were fine tuning an engine.

Can you imagine what it would be like if it's you who is desperate to keep those plates spinning and, at the same time, say, you are being constantly bombarded with rotten fruit from the audience, whilst the host stands over you pointing a loaded gun at your head? Full on pressure eh? Well that's what it feels like for Rob trying to create meals for paying customers.

There really is an art to cooking in a restaurant and we are discovering that in the most painful manner. Whilst Rob's already cooking an order for 4 meals, another one will come in. That's, potentially, 8 different meals he has to serve within 45 to 50 minutes, compounded by the fact that 15 minutes later another order for 4 meals can arrive.

Rob has to make sure the meals for each table are all ready at the same time, plating them and sending them out whilst still cooking the next order and so on, all within an acceptable time frame, for up to 40 people. Throw starters into the mix and the whole thing has the real possibility of going horribly, horribly wrong. It's enough to make anyone an absolute gibbering wreck. Compared to this, cooking for a dinner party (which is most people's experience of cooking en mass) is a piece of piss. The latter is as simple as making a sandwich whilst the former is like setting out to cook duck a l'orange for 40, when all the ducks are still alive and flapping around the kitchen.

I know you're thinking that, given the degree of difficulty, we've now discovered, of operating a catering kitchen we should have been more sympathetic to the tribulations of the ex-chef. But, in our defence, Chef had, supposedly, done it all before and should know what to do. After all, ours is not the first establishment he's worked in to offer food. He'd been doing it already for quite some time and, in fact, had been to college to learn how. I think if you profess to be a professional chef then producing all the meals without losing your mind is part of your job description surely?

However, Rob doesn't have the benefit of any training or any experience, but amazingly, he is coping quite well. At least, I think he is, but Rob, in his quieter moments, is not so sure. But let's ignore that for the moment. The secret to success, you see, is in the planning. You start at the end. We've already established an acceptable time frame in which meals should arrive at the table, so working backwards, you plan a menu of dishes that doesn't take longer than 20 minutes to cook and that all work if you have to cook them together. For example you can cook two meals at once if one of them can be prepared on the stove and one in the combi-oven. More complicated or slow-cook dishes, like lamb shanks, must be prepared in advance and then you have to work out a way of warming the meat up again, that doesn't destroy the dish during the heating up processes. This is quite simple if you have the right equipment, which we do.

In addition you have to make sure that everything you are going to need during the cooking session is already prepared. So it pays, to chop onions, make basic sauces, wash salad ingredients for garnishes, par-cook vegetables etc., all before you start the service. Then you have to arrange the kitchen utensils so things like pots and plates are easily to hand. You see, once you know how, it's quite easy.

It doesn't mean, however, that it's not stressful, because you're constantly having to think on your feet, managing what to do first and what to do next and then carry it out whilst you're planning further tasks. And you have to move extremely quickly in the kitchen to ensure everything is cooked enough, not burnt or under done, tastes nice and is piping hot when it goes out. And you have to keep this up for 3 or 4 hours at a stretch. Given the amount of physical activity and sweat it surprises me that you still get fat chefs.

Anyway, as I said, Rob is doing extremely well, after just two weeks practice. He's cooking some superb food and the feedback from the customers is excellent. Rob's also become adept at barking out orders like a sergeant major and is peppering the instructions with swearing and sarcasm just like Gordon Ramsay. The crucial difference being that Mr. Ramsey's got a raft of helpers in the kitchen whereas Rob just has Rory and a washer upper, so god knows what Gordon's got to swear about. The worst part about Rob's kitchen character, though, is the impatience. This following exchange is the type of thing that has been happening for a while now,

"How long will Table 8's meals be?" I enquired pleasantly.

"When the lamb's cooked," Rob barked back

"And when will that be?"

"When it's fucking cooked of course, stupid."

"But…?"

"Move. Don't stand there woman. You're in the way. Move. Move. Go away and come back in ten minutes"

So I give up, go out into the restaurant, clear a table or two and come back exactly ten minutes later. Taking my life in my hands, I ask,

"Are Table 8's meals ready yet?"

"I said they'd be ready in ten minutes and it's only been five, so what do you fucking well think?"

"Er..Actually it's been ten minutes."

"Does it look like I'm plating up Table 8's meals?"

"Um, not really," though it's hard to tell which table he's doing.

"So there's your answer then. Now, fucking hell, move out the way"

Of course, given this amount of downright rudeness and disrespect, I'm more than tempted to knife Rob with his best kitchen knife, but I don't, simply because I understand what has happened. Evil Twin has taken over and Evil Twin is necessary for Rob to get the job done. I wouldn't put up with Evil Twin in our everyday lives together, but as a method of coping in a highly tense and volatile situation, it's acceptable.

Mind you, Rob doesn't make it easy for me to survive the session. Under normal circumstances, if anyone spoke to me the way Rob does when Evil Twin is in control, I'd let him or her have it with both barrels, every time. Vile invective pours forth when I'm angry. I'm like a spitting, wild cat, much to Rob's amusement, not sensible, cogent or reasonable. So having to hold my tongue, constantly, puts me under extreme pressure too.

However, if I did make the mistake of biting back during an exchange with Rob like the one above, and many others besides, Rob would just stomp off there and then, because his nerves are on a knife edge and he's wound so tight as to nearly snap. And where would that leave us? I can't cook the bloody food.

So after a particularly scathing attack from someone I love intensely, I'm wounded and deeply hurt but, instead of asking for a hug, I just have to keep quiet, swallow my pride, wipe the welling tears from my eyes and pin a wobbly smile on my face as I walk out in to the restaurant. Because, you see, I've got customers who are paying good money to be fed and they really don't want to see me crying my eyes out because my husband's a bastard.

28. The Dotted Line   October 2006

I haven't really mentioned this much mainly due to the fact I would've ended up crying whilst I type, but for over four months we have been in the clutches of sobbing frustration because there has been no end in sight to the pub purchase. The delay has dragged on and on and on. At times, it seemed more likely, the whole thing would fall through than we should actually complete. And then where would we be, with no income and no-where to live? Wanting something to happen so desperately, and then finding out each day we are no further forward than the day before has caused us outrage and despair that really is constant. Rob has spent the last four months or so frequently screaming down the phone to incompetents. Evil Twin has escaped from the kitchen and is controlling the purchase of our pub. Sadly, Evil Twin is also rearing his ugly head in our day-to-day dealings with each other as well. Rob keeps shouting at me. But that's by the by.

So, with a great deal of pleasure and not a small amount of relief, I can thankfully say the incredibly long and hard fought battle is over. Today we completed. The pub is ours.

Of course, now it's over it's all a bit of an anti-climax. We've already opened the box and seen what's inside and, to be honest, it's a touch disappointing, like discovering the large and ornately wrapped Christmas present contains only birdseed and daffodil bulbs.

Given the fact Rob has discovered a talent for large-scale blagging, a tiny bit of us was half hoping the pub purchase would drag on for a bit longer. Who knows how far we could exploit the PubCo's embarrassment? A new kitchen, new furniture or, and this would deeply test their ingenuity – new, high-spending customers? But at what cost I wonder? How many times would Evil Twin have to pay us a visit?

I suppose it's too late now for reflecting on missed opportunities, but whilst there are many things we've gained in having a pub, like food and beer on tap, so to speak, there is something I've lost which is very important to me – my freedom.

My son left the other day to begin a new life in Southampton. He wasn't living with us and hadn't for some years, but he lived close and for the last four months he's been regularly popping in to see us (what am I saying? I mean - to eat and drink for free of course). On the odd occasion, when we were desperate, he's also helped out in the kitchen or behind the bar, and he's of an age where pub going is an attractive 7-nights-a-week activity, so his feedback on other pubs was very useful. It feels like my son's here, if not in body then certainly in spirit and, really, I can see him any time I like. But last weekend he packed up his car and came round to say goodbye.

His girlfriend lives in Southampton and it became a simple matter of either she moves up here or he moves down there and she won. So my son is going to a new flat, a new job and a new life without me in Southampton. And that makes me feel extremely sad. We've been through a lot my son and I, because, for many years I was a single parent and I like to think we've muddled through it all together with only a few hiccoughs along the way.

My son has endured the vagaries of my life at university and my career in marketing along with a first husband (and now a second one) and too many house moves to count. Maybe our constant moving has left him with itchy feet as he's moved out a few times before, to go to University himself or stay with other people for a bit, but this time, it's different. I know he won't be back for a long while because I think this may be the start of him settling down, carving out a life for himself in a new place. My son is not going to want to visit me that often, Southampton's a long way away and, worst of all, I really don't know how long it will be before I can visit him. Because, you see, I'm trapped in a pub.

Every night I'm either working or, if it's a precious night off, hiding from the customers, because the door to our private flat opens into the bar. If my leisure hours coincide with the pub being open then the last thing I usually want to do is show my face so I'm practically imprisoned up there, having to listen to the constant loud rumbles of the potato harvesting lorries as they speed past at this time of year, unless I want put my war paint on, get dressed into something more presentable than 10 year old pyjamas and emerge into the bar to brave my public. And if I do, of course, I have to talk to them.

Don't get me wrong, I like my customers, I really do (well, most of them), but there are times, because I'm essentially a private person, when I do need a bit of quiet time to myself. Times when I don't want to hear that Sasha's horse threw a shoe in a show, or Pinkie Moffit's lights aren't working and they can't be fixed until a week next Tuesday or the cricket Team has won a game or that Jim Carlisle's wife has run off with the window cleaner. Oh, wait a minute. Actually, I do want to know when someone's other half runs off with a tradesman. But the rest of it? On my night off I don't want to hear it.

So my freedom is practically non-existent, the surreptitious price you pay for running a pub. And I think it's a high price. No popping out with my girlfriend's for a spot of lunch. No jetting off to Majorca for a few days of sunshine. No attending family celebrations. The pub comes first and foremost and your life, and that of your family, just has to fit in around it. Of course you can go to these events if you can get someone to cover your shift, which is a bit easier for me because I only serve behind the bar and waitress, but for Rob, it's impossible. Rob's talents are the cornerstones of our business. There is absolutely no one we can trust to replace him in the kitchen, even for a few hours. And even if I do manage to find someone to work instead of me, I still have to be back to do the cashing up and put the day's takings in the safe, so getting even mildly drunk is entirely out of the question if I want to make any sense at all of the money we've made.

So I'm afraid our families and friends are forced to understand that we can't always attend a christening, a wedding or a 40th birthday party and I have to bear the shame and ignominy of disappointing them. It's not easy, I can tell you.

Of course the rewards are great. Knowing that people choose to come in our pub for a drink night after night or regularly pop in for a meal or travel from the other side of Hereford to try us out is extremely satisfying and I understand the reason everyone wants to tell me all about their lives is because usually I'm friendly and enquiring and ask them plenty of questions. I can't expect them to realise that I do need a rest from it every now and then, because when they are in my pub it is their down time and they want to socialise, not skulk about and ignore people as I like to do on my night off.

Genuinely, I'm pleased we have completed and the pub is now ours. We can mentally move on and stop having to fight and struggle with solicitors everyday. At least now, the pub has an intrinsic value to us. It's an investment and if we're very lucky and work very, very hard we should be able to sell the lease and the goodwill for more than we paid for it. At the end of the day our blood, sweat and tears, will pay off, in hard cash. And in the meantime we can enjoy what we are trying to build.

So, this evening, we had an impromptu party to celebrate. God knows how word got round so quickly, but the jungle drums must have been working over time because we were exceedingly busy. The beer flowed, all those with the drunken munchies devoured free food, warm congratulations hung in the air like a fog and Maurice, with the musical tastes of a 12 year old girl and after quite a few pints, warbled his way loudly through Westlife and Take That songs.

I couldn't help stopping at one point to quietly reflect, because it was that sort of evening. Pub life was certainly not what I'd expected. I thought it would be much easier than this for a start. But the pub was now ours and for that I was grateful. At least for a while.

I glanced across at Rob who was swigging a pint of Guinness and laughing loudly at something Maurice had said. My husband looked happy and I was pleased he was managing to relax a bit and enjoy himself. Then I noticed how his jeans were all bunched up around the middle, where he'd pulled his belt in tight in order to hold his trousers up. My husband had never looked so thin. This really shocked me.

"Bloody Hell," I thought. "What are we doing to ourselves?

29. The Refurb   October 2006

So now the pub is ours we've decided to refurbish, but having discovered years ago that Rob has an innate inability to throw anything away, I'm a little bit worried we'll end up with the same amount of old tat we had at the beginning.

There must be a hoarding gene I reckon. A single chromosome, if present on a hidden strand of DNA, compels you to keep forever the trophy you won for spelling at 6 years of age or the plastic figure from a cereal packet because your first boyfriend gave it to you. Or, in the case of my husband, every spare bit of wood, nails, screws or plastic he can find. To be squirreled away in the dark recesses of the shed, just in case. We have old LP's in there that are so warped and scratched they're only fit for stubbing cigarettes out on (I'm assuming there's a stack of 70's porn in there too – doesn't every man's shed have one on a shelf somewhere?). Nonetheless, we have to keep those useless vinyl records. God knows why. We don't even have a turntable to play them on. Does anyone these days?

A friend of mine horded so much kitchen equipment that the simple act of opening a cupboard meant you risked being buried alive. In each was a wall of stuff, precariously wedged in. There were bowls, cups, saucers, eggcups, Pyrex dishes, plastic dishes, plates, mugs, ramekins, measuring jugs, cheese graters, and all manner of kit. There was even a handy little gadget for leaving messages on toast. To even think of burning "I love you" onto your husband's breakfast is bad enough, but to actually pay money for a device that does it, then I suggest you need to put on this nice jacket and let a man in a white coat tie the arms round the back.

The altogether most surprising thing about the hoarding of all this kitchen equipment was that my friend couldn't cook. She just didn't know how, had never learned and invariably ate out. Perhaps she thought buying all the utensils would miraculously infuse her with the ability to prepare nourishing and tasty meals. Who knows?

Be that as it may, there are some of us, like me in fact, who are extremely good at culling the clutter of our lives. Excising the detritus of my every day existence is a breeze. A clear out of old clothes, shoes and costume jewellery is a bi-yearly activity, approached with gusto, carried out with glee and packed off unregrettably to one or other of the local charity shops. My rule of thumb is if I haven't worn it, used it or even seen it in the last year then it's going. If it's been proven that I don't need it or particularly want it, it's all sent away to be recycled. Given my enthusiastic approach to throwing away items that have outlasted their usefulness, I tell Rob to just tread carefully.

So, I'm approaching the prospect of a revamp with a great deal of relish. It's the perfect opportunity to de-tat the whole place and I know I'm going to enjoy it immensely. The ex-landlord has filled the pub with so much paraphernalia it looks like a house I visited once. There was so much mess in every room, jumble piled high on every flat surface including the floor, the owner had to clear a pathway from the front door to the kitchen along with a tight space around each important piece of furniture like the TV or the sofa. How do people live like that? If it wasn't for the fact I started sneezing as soon as my foot was over the threshold, I'd have lectured her about the benefits of culling your possessions and shown her how easy it was to put things into black bags and leave them out for the bin men.

The pub, perhaps, is not so bad, but a lot of this newly acquired stuff has no place at all in a hostelry that serves alcohol. Like the large, freestanding Laurel and Hardy statues, the leaping dolphin figurine, the dusty, dried flower arrangements, the vintage oil can, the mirror covered in a painted map of the UK, the trinket boxes. I could go on.

So with clear shelves in mind, today I have completely de-cluttered and Rob has helped (against my better judgement, mind you, what with his predilection for keeping everything). We managed to fill a whole skip full of junk, with only a few arguments over what to keep and what to throw away and the place now looks absolutely amazing. Bigger, tidier and much less like the home of a really old, mad person. There were some gems I did keep though, like a few horse brasses and a couple of superb warming pans. I'm not a complete philistine you know. Now, the next task is to paint.

I've said before the pub is only tiny, but viewing it without all the debris has made me realise to paint it all in one go is a really big job. The bottom of the restaurant is not too bad because the beamed ceilings are low, the same for the public bar, but there's a bit in the middle, the bit I call 'top restaurant' that has an unusually lofty ceiling and large windows for a 17th century building.

Today Rob and I stood in 'top restaurant' pondering on the time and effort it would require to do the painting ourselves. We decided to get someone in. I'm now in that enviable position of being able to decide the décor - tasteful, of course, and issue instructions to someone else to do the donkeywork. This has never happened to me in my life before. By that I mean having someone else do the painting rather than not being able to decide on what is tasteful.

Mind you, Taste is a strange thing. And even though taste is quite subjective everyone thinks they have it. But what can seem suitably stylish to one person is completely tacky to another. Once a friend of ours bought an antique-style world map to adorn the walls of his new flat. So far, so good. But the main cities of the world were picked out in coloured glass to look like precious stones. It was hideous and was only overshadowed by the reproduction 19th century hostess trolley he kept his post on. His clothes were the same. Expensive, electric-hued bits of what looked like old rags. Rob reckoned his friend wore unfeasibly colourful clothes for someone still living as a heterosexual.

In fact, taste seems to decline in direct ratio to how rich you are and our friend was quite wealthy. I've certainly seen some incredibly vulgar things in the homes of people who should know better, but are able to throw cash at it. Thankfully, Rob and I should always have impeccable taste, because we'll sure as hell never have any money.

So, tastefully improving the décor in the pub is our main objective. And if taste can be measured by the proportion of people who agree with you then that shouldn't prove too difficult to achieve because, to a man, all our customers concur - the existing décor has just got to go. The vast swathes of orange, the blinding light, the contract flooring, the dirty, nicotine-stained, white woodchip in the public bar - everything needs a complete overhaul.

So what style are we going for? Successful pubs, it seems to me, are ones that tap in to our nation's current penchant for all things historical. So, given ours is over 400 years old, ideally, the pub needs to go back to its roots. It needs to convey a sense of the past, a testament to its heritage as well as being warm and inviting. It needs to look authentic, as if you've just stepped into the 17th Century, but without being uncomfortable or unwelcoming.

A perfect example of the kind of thing I'm thinking of is a fantastic pub called The Fleece in Bretforton, Worcestershire. This inn has 'ancient' pub written all over it. For a start, it really is an old pub, which helps. Although it's no older than our own pub, the difference is, inside, it does look completely untouched by the last 400 years. The original flagstones are rubbed to a gentle patina by centuries' worth of feet and the furniture, fittings and ornaments would not have looked out of place in Anne Hathaway's cottage. To step into this pub is to step back in time. Which appeals to me enormously and would be a perfect design for our pub, complementing exactly, some of the locals, who look as if they've been coming in since the place was built.

There is only one slight problem, however. To accomplish my desired décor, would mean re-laying the floors, replacing internal doors, sandblasting beams, knocking down walls and filling the pub with antiques, all of which we do not have the budget for.

Ideally our pub needs to be gutted and turned over to the 17th Century equivalent of Laurence Llewlyn Bowen for a complete makeover, but we only have about £2.50 to spend so we're stuffed.

We will just have to do the best job we can and hope that's good enough. Mind you, any change at all would be an improvement, but at the very least the pub will look much fresher. The only real challenge I can foresee is to make sure Rob doesn't 'recycle' everything we've recently thrown away by bringing it back in the pub. I caught him lurking by that skip of junk earlier. It seems the hoarding gene is proving very hard to resist. Step away from the skip, Rob if you know what's good for you.

30. The Refurb – Part 2   October 2006

The redecoration of the pub is moving on apace and is severely trying my patience. We've managed to find a decorator who's motored ahead with efficiency and reliability. He even vacuums up after himself at the end of the day. So, it's not the decorator who's annoying me particularly because he is conscious of our peculiar circumstances and has fitted in around us very well.

Incidentally, the decorator is quite attractive but talks with an Essex accent and that quite effectively quashes every little bit of any lurking ardour I may have. I'm not saying there's anything wrong with Essex accents, or any accent for that matter (except, perhaps, Birmingham ones, and I can say that with impunity because I'm from Birmingham originally), it's just that I find accent-less voices much more sexy. The deep, soothing tones of Received Pronunciation is for me the stuff of fantasies. I'd take Richard E Grant, over David Beckham any day of the week.

No, the redecoration of the pub is irksome because; predictably, the regular customers showed their usual tolerance and consideration throughout the process and have complained bitterly about all the upheaval. Apparently I should have decorated throughout the night so as not to disrupt their routines. After spending the first week telling Rob and myself in minute detail what was wrong with the pub they are now irritated because we are altering it and, as usual, are highly vocal in their dissent. I think they are probably a bit worried about the impending modifications. I've come to understand change is not necessarily viewed as a good thing. It doesn't even matter if the change is for the better. Change is bad, any change at all. I've even had adverse comments to new brands of crisps. People do like to feel safe and protected in well-established routines. Oh well, it's just a bit of paint. They'll get used to it.

We asked the decorator to start in the restaurant, we figured the biggest job should be done first, and we shut that room for two days whilst the walls and the woodwork were painted. By the way, we chose for our tasteful refurbishment, deep red and cream. I wanted to use flat, chalky Farrow & Ball emulsion, but we couldn't afford it, so the decorator took the original paint chart with my chosen colours on to some magical emporium somewhere and got them to mix up a batch of trade paint that matches my choices exactly. Well almost. Rather than have a coloured feature wall we've painted half the room in cream and half in red. Not striped. That would be silly. Instead we've painted two of the opposing walls in one colour and the remaining two in the other. Looking at it all now it's been done, I reckon we made a really good choice. It's warm and welcoming and looks, dare I say it, a little bit classy.

Perhaps this is another thing that's worrying the locals. Before they felt comfortable in the bar because any mud smeared across the floor or caked on the barstools didn't really matter. It's a working farmer's pub so they could gleefully traipse a bit of wet mud in knowing they won't get in to trouble or feel out of place.

There is only one farmer who takes his boots off when he comes in and leaves them by the front door. The rest of them don't really give a shit. Mud is a fact of life in these parts, a given constant, like the rain. What the regulars don't realise yet is, even though it's now been decorated, they can still drag mud through the bar. I don't mind.

Anyway we appear to have divided opinion. "Why are the walls painted in different colours?" was one of the tamer comments. How do you explain mood creation and other theories of interior design to a rough and ready man-of-the-land?

I tried "Because it adds a bit of character to an otherwise flat room and breaks up the expanse of colour. If it were all red it would be too dark and if it were all cream it would be too bright. I'm trying to add a bit of character, make a statement, stop it all looking a bit uniform."

"Oh". The farmer nodded, but didn't look convinced. Oh well, I know what I'm talking about even if no one else does.

It has taken another two days to paint the public bar and a further day to 'dress' the whole pub. This involved Rob and I primping and plumping, tidying and tweaking, moving countless small objects to one place, carefully considering them from all angles, having a bit of a row, moving them to another place and deliberating all over again. If anyone knows why this last activity should be assisted by leaning your head to one side and then another, whilst staring, saucer-eyed at the object, would you please tell me?

I have spent the eye-popping amount, according to Rob, of £300 on cushions, searched high and low for cheap curtains that look expensive, fiddled about with pinecones and fake fruit to create interesting displays whilst Rob has drilled holes in impenetrable masonry to put up pictures. I have polished second hand condiment sets we bought from a pub clearance sale, artfully arranged table decorations and draped the back of the leather Chesterfield with a fake sheepskin rug.

We have inexpertly recovered an old bench with some upholstery material picked up for £3 a metre and, after careful consideration, chose to completely ignore the poor state of the rickety dining room tables. Stripping the lot of them with varnish remover then sanding, waxing and buffing was an option. But there are at least 10 tables. Restoring them would take far too long. Instead, we've just screwed the legs back on properly. Listen, I don't have the time to even eat, let alone refurbish wobbly, old tables.

We arranged second-hand, squashy tub chairs around an occasional table in the restaurant to replace the wooden, bum numbing ones we bought with the pub and covered up the worst of the plaster with a bedspread I made years ago. It's meant to look like a tapestry wall hanging and does if you squint.

I'm grateful to Rob's late grandmother who bought a deep-stained, wooden Old Charm dresser in the 60's, which Rob inherited. We have cannibalised it for restaurant use as a dumb waiter, to replace the flimsy and decidedly distasteful piece of melamine and chipboard furniture we used before.

We have moved furniture around so many times I think I have may have a hernia. In total, we have spent about £3,500 and our pub looks acceptable. It doesn't look fantastic, but it certainly looks better than it did. God knows how much the big companies must spend when they refurbish a pub. I dread to think.

We could have carried on haemorrhaging money in a futile attempt to authentically re-create a 17th century country pub. But we do not have the money to do it properly, so we've attempted "Shabby Chic" instead. Which is an optimistic way of describing scratched and battered furniture in the vain hope people will believe it's meant to be like that.

As I said, our budget was tiny and we ran out of money long before everything that needed to be sorted was so. I desperately wanted to do something about the horrible lighting in the bar. When Ex-landlord took over the pub in the first place he, unwisely, had all the wall lights in the public bar ripped out and replaced with ceiling saucers responsible for that searingly brilliant light I may have already mentioned. We wanted to re-install the originals on the wall to create a suitably dim and moody ambience. But oh, the cost. Instead we left the ceiling saucers as they were and just removed some of the bulbs. And, because we've also installed low wattage bulbs in the remainder, the bar is quite authentically gloomy now, much darker, in fact, with filmy pools of light. Much more atmospheric. Perfect.

In the evening glow, the whole pub looks lovely. We've refreshed the place completely and, at the same time, created somewhere that seems warm and cosy. Tonight, we launched the new look on our unsuspecting customers. I wanted to gloat. I wanted to hear the wondrous oohs and aahs and receive praise at our ingenuity. I wanted to be complimented on our impeccable taste and cunning use of inexpensive soft furnishings. I wanted to bask in the glory of a job well done.

Instead, we get:

"Hey, it's a bit dark in here. I can't see whether you've given me the right change."

31. The Christmas Party   December 2006

One of our regular customers really boosted my self-esteem the other day. I was putting on my big, woolly, ankle-length, winter coat prior to popping outside to collect some empty glasses.

"Do you know," said my customer "That coat improves your figure no end". I smiled sweetly - and then punched him in the face.

I was relating this tale to Rob afterwards and he said "You didn't really punch him in the face?"

"No, I didn't,' I replied, "but I wanted to. The cheek of the man. What I should have said to him, of course, is you can never be too thin, according to Wallis Simpson." I laughed.

Rob pondered on this for a second or two then said, " Hmm, yes, but I can sort of see what he means" and with that he squeezed my shoulder manfully and wandered off to chop something in the kitchen, wiping the smile off my face as he went. Before the pub I'd have got a hug and been told how beautiful I was. Now he just agrees with my detractors.

Still, my appearance is not the most pressing thing I've got to worry about at the moment. The most immediate is how I'm going to get through December without fading completely. We have so many Christmas parties booked in the restaurant, I'm very pleased to say, that our pub will be buzzing and the money trickling in a bit faster than usual.

In the 24 days (minus non-food days), up to Christmas Eve we've about 29 parties booked, including some "shoot dinners'. Now this may not seem a lot to the hardened licensed trade experts out there, but to Rob and myself it gives us a rather smug, warm glow. I'm pleased and more than a little amazed that 29 people have decided to spend their Christmas cash with us and, depending on how large their booking is, at least 6 of their friends, colleagues or families have too. Isn't that some validation we're doing ok? It's either that or the fact we're cheaper than every one else.

A week into December and with about 13 parties under my belt already I've tried my hardest to make each one lively and fun, with my best hostess manner. Thankfully, I can do this because now I'm in my (ahem) middle 40's I have boundless self-assurance that was completely absent in my 20's.

Back then I was woefully shy. So reserved, in fact, there were plenty of times an evening was spent with my girlfriends in a pub where I never uttered a word. My lack of confidence was such I was convinced, opening my mouth would result in a) No one hearing me or b) Everyone thinking my utterances were not worth the effort of listening. It was quite awful I can tell you.

I'm unrecognisable now from that timid, tongue-tied youngster. I am the master (mistress?) of small talk. In our pub I can instigate a conversation with a bar full of strangers with no problem at all and there have even been times, when I have actually managed to make a group of customers laugh. It took until the beginning of my thirties for my confidence to emerge, which meant my entire 20's were spent in an agony of self-consciousness.

The difference a big dollop of self-assurance has made to my life is immeasurable; especially as your forties is an in-between age. I'm not really young, but not old either. Being hybrid, it's a bit hard to know how to dress and what to do with your hair and make-up because the changes to your body seem to happen on a daily basis. Wrinkles develop overnight and the extra fat pounds creep on until one day, the person looking back at you in the mirror is not the person you see in your mind's eye (in my head I look 34, but we won't dwell on that).

It doesn't bother me too much though. To grow old gracefully you have to be comfortable in your own skin. And this is really what being in my forties has done for me. Building my confidence since my thirties, I am now a defined person, with specific likes and dislikes and able to voice an opinion. I can conquer anything, am strong, resourceful and resilient, with much more energy.

I love being in my forties. So what if short skirts are out because my knees are chubby. So what if my boobs have drooped and my hair is going grey. Being this age means knowing how to deal with it both mentally and with support garments and hair dye.

Of course, these days I come into contact with a far greater number of the general public than before and, whilst my confidence is at a level which easily deceives me in to thinking how great I am, serving in the pub has bought home to me how much less attractive I am than I used to be. I've always liked flirting, but not had much opportunity to do so, what with working in an office alongside Rob for the best part of the last 10 years. So you can imagine how pleased I was when I realised I could flirt to my heart's content with some of the good-looking young men who frequent the bar, it's harmless and, what I consider to be, a perk of the job.

Only I keep forgetting, now I'm older and because I've lost quite a bit of weight, my face is sliding downwards. For these poor boys it must be like being chatted up by your mum.

That explains the uncomfortable expressions.

Most people, as they grow older, look the same only swollen (Chubbing Up, as my friend Rachel calls it), but I've found a foolproof way to shed a stone and half in 6 months, whilst eating as much chocolate and as many bags of crisps and chips as you like. It's the best diet around though a bit expensive, but it certainly works. All you have to do is – buy a pub. It's as simple as that. You'll be thin, but decidedly unhealthy, although I'm not altogether sure that would worry most women.

I do know I'm getting old, and it really doesn't bother me, but I'm not looking forward to becoming even more forgetful than I am now or losing my hearing or the control of my bladder. Before too long I'll be sitting in my wheelchair, reflecting on how jolly it was to be a publican and having to lean sideways to gently fart. My status in life will be shot to pieces and anyone younger who speaks to me will be patronizing and loud. Getting older is not so bad, but actually being old? Oh joy.

Still, hopefully that's a long way off yet. At the moment I am confident, bright and bubbly, even though I look a bit crumpled at times, and I can easily join in with, or even lead, all the joking and bonhomie at the Christmas parties we've got booked. Albeit I've told the same joke millions of times.

I can't remember jokes so I try vainly to hang on to the details of just one and when I've told everyone that I'll try and remember another one. The current joke is:

An English man goes into a Dublin pub and asks an old Irish bloke at the bar what the quickest way to Cork would be.

"Are ye walking or travelling by car?" says the Irish chap

"By car" said the Englishman

The Irishman pauses to give the matter some thought then replies,

"Aye, that'd be the quickest way then".

Don't knock it. The joke has to be simple so I can bloody remember it. And most people laugh, but that may be because of my fake Irish accent. Who cares as long as they find it funny?

The Christmas parties and shoot dinners have been raucous affairs so far. Our pub is rocking and everyone appears to enjoy themselves. Yesterday, though, I had one of the most subdued works gatherings I've ever come across. Each person was very, very quiet, and detached, even the one young bloke with them, who downed copious amounts of rum and black wasn't loud, just swayed a bit. Extremely worried they were dissatisfied with the food or the pub or me, I tried my joke and all it elicited was a faintly embarrassed titter. I was surprised. Don't they appreciate a splendid joke when they hear one? They ate their meals and pulled their crackers, but didn't linger.

I thought, as they left, it wouldn't be a great deal of fun working in that company, but the reason for their passivity, I found out later, was most of them had been made redundant the week before. Under the circumstances, I think the young chap who got quietly pissed had the right idea. I'd have done the same if I didn't think the drink would make my ageing face slide downwards that little bit faster.

32. The Lost Licence   December 2006

Crikey. Our pub is cold. One of the disadvantages of a timber frame building is the lack of insulation. Combine that with the draughts and the single-glazed windows and it's costing nearly £1,000 a month in gas and electricity. But I must have it warm. Cold pubs are cheerless places. They have to be cosy otherwise people won't stay. So I have to have the heating on most of the time in order to even take the chill off. I've also lit the fire in the bar, but I only keep it going in the evenings as its eating logs. The expense is huge. It's also a bit of a bone of contention because the early drinkers insist on a fire and, whilst I try to be accommodating, for me it's another chore to be done before I can open at 6 o'clock. Sometimes people drive me mad.

Rob and I have realised that meeting people's expectations is a constantly moving goal. You provide them with little, hopefully unexpected, niceties, like free food on the bar, or buy them a pint every now and then or let them drink a little later than usual or, indeed, light a fire and at first, they are appreciative and grateful. But after a while they come to demand it as a right and then you have to disappoint them if you say no or if you always say yes, have to think of something extra that will excite them when the original things have become the norm.

I understand, these days, being a good publican is about not just meeting your customers' expectations, but exceeding them. However, in a small, family-run pub such as ours the persistent presumption is very wearing. I feel like I'm always running to catch up and never quite making it. Is this normal?

I've noticed, though, that whilst we never get any praise, what we do get is a continual stream of visitors and this has to be enough of an indication that we're doing ok. One of our regulars is a very grumpy, retired professional and nothing we ever do seems to impress him. He's not opinionated, just cynical and I can appreciate he's old enough to have seen it all before. For this reason it pleases me when he appears each evening, in the restaurant side, which is now completely non-smoking, to drink a couple of pints of Hancocks and do the crossword in the Times we buy each day. He only lives across the road and according to his wife, he enjoys popping across to the pub at 10pm for an hour or so. It's a new activity for him, one we've had a hand in because we provide the two things that bring him comfort, good beer and the Times crossword. I suppose it's these little things that count and I'm really pleased we've made a difference to someone's life, no matter how small.

I watch our regulars with interest sometimes. Contrary to what you may think, there are no stereotypes here. No country yokels that conform to your idea of what rural people are like. They are all individual, some with differing circumstances and some similar. There are a few farmers who are exceedingly entrepreneurial, whilst there are others that refuse to accept the passing of the old ways, although these are definitely in the minority. If any are really struggling then it's hard to tell, although whilst one will diversify to make the most of his land, considering setting up livery stables or Pick-Your-Own fruit or, in one case I heard of, setting up a mountain board centre on a hill he happened to have, another will just carry on with less and less income as each year goes by.

Many are passionate about what they do, but it's a sad fact not many of them can do it anymore. Take dairy farmers, for example. There are few dairy herds left around here, and that's because, according to DEFRA, The average cost of milk production is around 21p per litre whilst the farmers can only sell it for just 18p per litre. It doesn't take a genius to work out that's a deficit of 3p per litre. No wonder there are hardly any dairy cows left in our area.

Even if farmers have the foresight and wherewithal to diversify, it doesn't mean their neighbours will allow it. If a farmer is close to what I call an 'incomer', then the farmer and the incomer are viewing the surrounding land from very different perspectives. As I think I may have said before, Herefordshire is working country and the land is a by-product of the industry that goes on in it. But not according to incomers it isn't. Incomers have a perceived view that the countryside should look like that described in "Cider With Rosie" by Laurie Lee. Admittedly, the book is a wonderfully nostalgic view of rural living at the end of the First World War, but as a template for rural living in the noughties, then it really does leave a lot to be desired.

Incomers want the countryside to be neat, clean, romantic and, above all picturesque. There's no getting away from the fact that farms can be untidy, noisy and covered in mud which spills out all over the road. Incomers want rolling green fields, with neat hedgerows, quiet country lanes and no cattle that'll chase their dog when they go for a walk. But farmers deal in muck and mud and, often, the incomers complain bitterly about it. It doesn't stop the incomers buying up the property though, probably because they are wearing inch-thick rose coloured glasses at first. As soon as a small, detached cottage becomes available they circle like vultures, purchasing with a view to making the house bigger, neater and more valuable, increasing the worth of the properties in the area until they are way beyond anything the born and bred locals can afford.

I'm generalising, of course, but you get the idea. I'm an incomer myself, but I try really hard to fit in rather than make everyone else mould around some idealised view I have of country living. It's about getting to know your neighbours well and learning how best to get on with them rather than the other way round. We tried this long before we ever took over the village pub. Rob even helped with the sheep shearing last year. It very nearly killed him.

Farmers and incomers are not the only ones who worry me. I'm also concerned about some of the youngsters around here. There is a well-established local authority housing estate just up the road from us and, of course, a few of the 20 year olds drink in the pub, and a nice bunch they are too. Nonetheless, to a man (albeit young man), they seem to have little or no further education and almost non-existent ambition. They must surely be the products of a Herefordshire education and, if this is the case, then Herefordshire should be trying harder. These youngsters have not been inspired to think in terms of having a career, just a job and whilst it's laudable that most earn good livings it's sad they have not been given the tools to make a future for themselves beyond what they are doing now.

I'm not knocking them at all and Rob and I have spent many an uproarious night in their company. No, I'm just a bit sad because all of them are capable of so much more if only their potential could be realised.

One of them in particular is a quiet, individual who often occupies the grey areas on the edge of the crowd. He knows the others well as they've all grown up together, but is often the butt of the jokes and the piss taking. I hope this doesn't upset him. If an unsuspecting single, young female comes in the pub (usually one of our staff) he tries to monopolise them, constantly following them about and trying to buy them drinks. Short of dry humping their legs he couldn't make it any more obvious he fancies them. Inevitably he annoys them and, in a fit of pique, gets drunk, storms out of the pub and does something really stupid. Happens every time.

Recently, he took his mum and dad's car and crashed it on the main Hereford to Worcester road. He sat in a drunken stupor in the vehicle until the police arrived, was duly arrested, charged and prosecuted and received 1500 hrs community service and a 2 year driving ban. Oh, and of course a police record.

For a while he's really fucked up his life. I'm assuming he realises that and I'm hoping it will make a difference to him for the future. He really is a nice lad. He deserves so much better.

There's not much I can do to help him, though. But in order to at least meet this customer's expectations I really should find him some nice young lass to go out with. I have many washer uppers who fit the criteria I suppose, but with regard to customer service in this instance, there's only so far I'm prepared to go and this chap, I'm afraid, is on his own.

33. The Job   December 2006

We've given a job to our love struck customer with the drink driving record. Well sort of. Love Struck helps out when we need an extra pair of hands and the good soul comes down to the pub every Saturday afternoon to cut the lawn. It turns out that the chap is reliable and conscientious, is friendly to the customers and is efficient behind the bar. Quite an asset in fact.

We've also given Michael a job. Michael is a young chap who comes in the pub at the weekend. Michael has been visiting on a Saturday night for a few months now. At first he just sat and watched as everyone enjoyed themselves, but gradually he worked his way in and now joins in and has a laugh with the rest of them. At least he tries to because Michael has a speech impediment so great he's almost unintelligible. I was hoping I'd get used to the way he talks and be able to understand him after a while, but it hasn't happened yet.

Michael's parents are farm workers and Michael does a few odd jobs here and there for the farmer his parents work for. I think people assume he's retarded, but I think the problem is he's just completely uneducated. It's hard to believe in this day and age, but I think Michael slipped through the net.

We managed to decipher that he's 28, but his writing is that of a 5 year old. Given he seems so bright and alert it's hard to believe his writing is so undeveloped because he has an inability to learn. More likely, I suspect, he just hasn't really been shown how. Similarly, his inability to communicate is so profound I wonder why he's not had speech therapy. Michael can be understood about 10% of the time, the rest just sounds like gibberish. We know he's trying to say something, but we just don't know what. If he's had a few pints then the stream of incomprehensible language just gets worse. I've never encountered anything like this before. Is this typical of living in the country? I can't believe so. I'm sure it was long ago they discovered that dyslexia, for example, was not just the child being stupid and refusing to read, so I know the education department's response to children's development problems is now both enlightened and informed. Michael's only just a bit older than my son so what can (or not) have happened?

Michael travels everywhere by pushbike and, I managed to understand the other day, he's been travelling on his bike from farm to farm for a few weeks now looking for work. But no one will give him a job. I'm not sure why. He says, I think, that he hates to be unemployed, so I've asked him to come down on Friday to be a sort of handyman around the pub.

We need someone to clean out the chickens, sweep the pavement outside the front door, clean the windowsills, water the plants and all sorts of horrible, but essential, little jobs like that we just don't have the time to do. Rob is trying to keep on top of it but having to do all that and work in the kitchen aswell is killing him. I know the tasks are menial, but they're the necessarily detail that makes the pub a welcoming place to be. I hope Michael doesn't mind and that he understands he'd be helping us enormously if he did those chores for us.

Michael is an extremely loveable chap and is rather sweet. No-one takes the piss out of him and the youngsters get him to join in whenever they can, whether it's playing darts, dancing along to CD's or just standing around chatting. Admittedly he doesn't do much of the latter, but he does listen and join in whenever he can.

Last Saturday, it was getting toward the end of the evening and we'd had a really good night. Loads of people in the restaurant eating, loads of people in the bar drinking, we really couldn't complain. Rob had finished cooking and was in the bar with all the regulars, coiffing a pint of Guinness or two and trying to unwind from a particularly busy session. As usual, I was behind the bar pulling a pint or two.

We were all listening to Maurice who was telling us that when his wife had a recent hysterectomy the surgeon found the watches of all her ex-boyfriends up there (you know where) and bought an assortment out on a tray to show him. Clare, Maurice's wife, had accompanied her husband to the pub on this occasion and was patiently waiting for him to finish having a laugh at her expense. She rolled her eyes at the implied promiscuity and said,

"For god's sake Maurice, don't make me laugh - it hurts". And everyone laughed even more with the two of them, always a reliable source of entertainment.

Clare retaliated by telling us that last week the two of them had gone out for a night on the town in Worcester with another couple. By the end of the evening, the two men were exceedingly pissed and arrived back in the village swaying alarmingly as they emerged from the taxi. Whilst staggering across the front lawn towards his house, Maurice was so inebriated he couldn't stand up and slumped down on the grass in a deep sleep. Now Maurice, as I've said before is 6ft 4in tall, a big bloke. His slightly less drunk friend, John, is a little bloke with glasses and no hair (looks a bit like Rob, actually).

John tried for a while to lift Maurice, tugging the large man's arm but couldn't budge him, so instead started to remove his friend's clothing. The two women had been watching the bladdered pair with amusement, but when John attempted to de-clothe Maurice in the open air Clare felt compelled to ask,

"John, why are you taking Maurice's clothes off?"

Huffing and puffing and red-faced with exertion, but having only managed to remove Maurice's socks and shoes, John explained.

"If he's got no clothes on he'll be lighter to lift, won't he?"

We all laughed and Maurice, who doesn't seem to have an embarrassment bone in his body, chuckled the loudest and the longest.

Whilst all this revelry was going on Michael must have slipped away quietly to go home, as usual, but as soon as he emerged from the pub saw a bunch of young lads legging it, having pinched his bike. Michael shouted at them loudly, but the lads just ran off with his only form of transport between them. All Michael could do was dart back into the pub to alert everyone to his dilemma. He was much distressed I can tell you, the poor boy.

As soon as they realised what had happened, Maurice and Rob abandoned their pints and shot out of the pub after the culprits. The whole bar crowded round the bay window to watch the two of them race down the road. Because Maurice was taking long strides as he ran, Rob's little arms and legs were pumping furiously trying to keep up. Maurice looked like Rocky Balboa on a training run and Rob looked like his pet midget. We watched till they disappeared round the bend in the road then all the remaining people in the bar turned their attention to Michael who was weeping and distraught about the theft of his bike.

Some time later, and as we were still trying to comfort Michael, a cheer went up as a dishevelled and puffed out Rob and a calm-as-you-like Maurice entered the bar. They were wheeling the bike. Michael was so pleased he gave each of them a hug and cycled off home happy.

Of course, pints were served all round to the last remaining 20 or so customers left in the pub whilst Maurice and Rob told us what had happened. I'm not going to relate the tale here, because all you need to know is Michael got his bike back safely. I can reveal, however, as I was told; when Maurice and Rob confronted the gang, one of them peed his pants. I can only assume the boy pissed himself laughing at the pair of them.

34. Christmas Day   December 2006

Our first Christmas Day and I opened the pub an hour early this morning, at 11am, not really knowing what to expect. A few people had said they'd be popping in for drinks to wish us all the good tidings of the season, but I didn't know whether we'd be busy or not. Last year at this pub the bar was packed and I presumed we'd see quite a few people too, but you never know. One thing I have learnt in the last few months is, in the main, people are strange and with the exception of a few, very unreliable.

When we woke this morning Rob and I realised we'd forgotten to buy each other presents. I'm not too fussed really because, now, to me, the purpose of Christmas is to make as much money as possible. Call me a philistine if you like, but I think you'll find that's mostly the point, otherwise why would some shops start displaying their Christmas stock at the end of August? In fact each year the Christmas 'push' seems to get earlier and earlier. I wonder why they don't dispense with the pretence altogether and just have Christmas all year round?

Actually, I lied there. I did buy Rob a present; he just didn't buy me one. He had been working so hard I thought it would be cruel to ignore the fact it was Christmas altogether so I bought him a couple of books, Gordon Ramsey's autobiography and Derren Brown's "Tricks of the Mind". I gave him the books before we opened the pub this morning. He unwrapped the packages with little excitement, and, when he saw what I'd bought him, viewed the gifts with as much disappointment as I surely conveyed when my parents, unprompted, gave me a suitcase as the main present for my 21st birthday (It wasn't as if I needed a big hint to leave home as I'd already left for college, so I can't imagine what they were trying to say).

Anyway, I digress. So here we were on Christmas morning, Rob opening presents and not looking very pleased about what he'd received.

"Don't you like them?" I asked

"Yes, of course I do."

"Well, what's the problem then?

"I thought we weren't going to bother buying each other presents this year?"

"It seemed a nice thing to do to surprise you"

"I haven't bought you anything"

"It doesn't matter. I can always read one of these books"

"I wish you'd told me you were buying me a present"

"It wouldn't have been a surprise then would it?"

"I feel bad now"

"I told you, it doesn't matter. Look, just consider these books as a present to both of us. Ok?"

"Ok"

And with that, Rob meandered off to make gravy.

Later, I unbolted the front door, not feeling overly festive, but prepared to appear so for the sake of my customers. One of our part-time bar staff had agreed to help this lunchtime until 1pm and others said they'd help if needed but at half past 11, with only 4 people in the bar, Sarah and I were passing the time discussing the worst Christmas present we'd ever received. I reckoned mine was a sandwich toaster bought by an old boyfriend and Sarah's was a large, green, concrete tortoise.

By 11.45 more people had trickled in and there was, at least, a gentle hum of bonhomie across the bar. We'd agreed our Christmas present to our adoring public would be a free first drink and a mince pie and by 12pm I think word had got round there was free beer at the pub because we were hit with a wave of eager customers all clamouring for a pint. It's a weird thing about free alcohol; it makes everyone the publican's friend, at least for as long as it takes them to drink it.

By 12.15 Sarah and I were drowning under the sheer weight of pub goers. They were a few deep at the bar, all waving money and trying to attract our intention in order to get served. The only way I had of deciding who to serve next was - did I recognise them? There was no way at all of telling who was first in the queue. Honestly, there were so many people packed in to our little bar there wasn't a credit card space between any of them. It was all very cosy. Strangely, there were quite a few people I'd never seen before, although the regulars seem to know them so I presumed they lived round here. I think it's odd when people go into their local pub only once a year. I get my teeth scraped at the dentist more often than that and believe me going to our pub is nicer.

Luckily one of our other part time bar staff turned up plus Love Struck. They both jumped behind the bar to help out and we managed to clear the backlog quite quickly, all bouncing off each other in our haste to serve in such a confined space. I was reminded fondly of our first night in the place, when Rob and I kept crashing into each other in a frantic bid to quickly serve all our new customers.

Around quarter to one, I watched a strange man in a cagoule trying to fight his way through the throng. As he approached I noticed he was wearing bicycle clips and I remember thinking how clever he was to cycle to the pub on Christmas Day and avoid any possibility he'd be tempted to drink and drive. I also thought he's more likely to be flattened by a dead donkey than to get pulled over by the police on today of all days, in the middle of the countryside, but I admired his caution.

The poor guy arrived at the bar looking somewhat flustered and asked me if I was the landlady.

"I am" I concurred

"Oh hello," he continued. "My colleagues and I are cycling for the day and I wonder if it's alright to eat our lunch here",

"Oh dear, I'm afraid we aren't serving lunch today, only to those who've booked"

"No, I mean, can we eat the lunch we've bought with us?"

I must have looked a little nonplussed at this because he quickly added

"Of course we'll all buy a drink".

Strangely amused I told him it would be alright, but I was afraid there wasn't much room to sit given the amount of people in the bar at that moment.

"Don't worry," he replied "We'll find somewhere to perch" And with that he turned round to fight his way back through the crowd to where he'd left 4 other similarly nylon-clad men, who were shifting nervously from foot to foot, ready to flee if someone so much as spoke to them.

True to his word they all bought a drink each. The only drink they did purchase in fact. And they were all soft drinks.

"What a wasted opportunity" I thought. "Assuming they are lonely and separate individuals who've sought each other out to endure together what is essentially considered to be a family day, I wonder why they just don't get rip-roaringly pissed".

I watched them extract their packed lunch from their nether regions (or so it seemed). Each of them had sandwiches all squashed up in cling film. It looked like they'd been sitting on them for the last 3 hours as the bread had cleaved to the shape of their buttocks. They gingerly peeled off the wrapping and munched their way through a meagre meal, stopping every now and then to sip the orange juice or the coke they so patently didn't want.

I wasn't sure whether to feel sorry for them or not, given that it was Christmas Day and all. But then I decided that they'd chosen this particular activity themselves when any sane person would have booked a table for 5 in a pub or restaurant and had a slap up meal along with a few bevvies, just as I planned to do with Rob and three or four well chosen guests this afternoon when we'd managed to get rid of all the drinkers and all the diners.

A passing thought ran through my head. Something had occurred to me that would explain it, especially their unseasonal disregard for the occasion. I wondered perhaps – were they Jehovah's Witnesses? Or did they think that a long cycle, broken only by a coke and a flattened sarnie in a pub was, indeed, a celebration? I didn't dwell on this thought for long though, because Maurice was up the corner doing his usual party trick of trying to balance a full pint on his head. The contents of that glass would, before long, be spilt over a wide radius of Christmas revellers, so I went to rescue it before I had a mess to clear up. Merry Christmas everyone.

35. New Year's Eve   December 2006

I've just left Rob upstairs, on the floor outside our bedroom. He's collapsed in a drunken heap and won't budge any further. He moans in protest every time I even so much as prod him with a finger, so I've covered him with a blanket and left him to it.

You can bet your bottom dollar he'll be suffering in the morning, cooking a roast in the kitchen with a grey face, a churning stomach and the smell of stale Guinness oozing from every pore.

Yup, last night was New Year's Eve and so, in order to a) give people an excuse to come to the pub and b) make a bit of money, we decided to host a party. And I can honestly say our New Year's Eve party, was a blast.

It's a funny thing, mind you, about this particular night of the year, that you always feel under pressure to celebrate the occasion in some way, even if you only plan to get pissed with a group of other individuals all desperate to have a good time.

I recall, it was even worse for the Millennium New Year's Eve. People were debating how to celebrate up to 6 months before. The pressure to do something zany and different was so great that Rob and I ended up not doing much mainly because there was too much to choose from. We could have gone to a fancy dress party in Stafford, a cocktail party in Finchley or joined the drunken masses in Centenary Square, Birmingham. And these were only the offers I can remember. There were plenty more. In the end we joined a group of walkers and yomped up the Malvern Hills in the dark, to light a beacon at the top.

With more than a passing nod to the occasion, we decided to take vodka and tonic with us in a 2-litre lemonade bottle, taking turns to quaff as we walked up the very steep hill. We huffed, puffed and drank our way to the top along with at least 50 other people. I hate to walk slowly, so we marched up the track, overtaking some of the slower participants and looking, for the all world as if we were trying to cover, say, 26 miles before daybreak. On reaching the top (1395ft) Rob and I congregated eagerly with the others around a brazier, which was on top of a high pole.

I was looking forward to the lighting. There was something quite primeval about the idea of it and it was definitely different. To be able to say we'd seen in the new millennium by standing on a very high hill round a fire was more than a little enterprising, I thought. And cheap.

I watched a man climb on to a raised podium from where he reached up and set fire to the beacon. We all oohed and aahed. It was magnificent. I looked over at Rob (well at the two Rob's I was seeing. It was quite pleasing, I can tell you) with warmth and contentment in my heart. All was well with the world and a bright future for us both lay ahead. Then the man, who was still on the podium, opened a large book. Everyone gathered in closer to hear what he had to say, staring up at this chap in wonder. I was beginning to feel a bit uncomfortable at this point, simply because my head was swimming and I had a sudden urgent desire to lie down. I've never been one for drinking and the alcohol was making me light-headed. Luckily, the squash of the crowd held me upright, and Rob, of course.

In the light of the flames, the man started speaking.

"We thank God for the…"

Rob and I looked at each other in horror. We'd inadvertently stumbled into a nest of God-botherers. How did that happen? Our senses are normally alive to this sort of thing, meaning we can avoid them like the plague. It was impossible to leave because of the number of people crowding around us so we stood there waiting for the bloke to finish. He droned on for about 15 minutes. I tuned out after the first 5 and spent the rest of the time thinking how hungry I was.

Eventually we lost patience. Why is it that all ecclesiastical members insist on relating everything to god or Jesus no matter how tenuous the link? You can just imagine any church service can't you? "I like pizza with just cheese on, but I know there are other flavours you can choose from. You can have some with bits of chicken on and some with spicy beef. In fact, pizza is a bit like God…" Know what I mean?

So, as soon as was humanly possible, Rob and I ran away, legging it back down the hill. It took us double the amount of time to reach the bottom than it had taken to climb because I was so rat-arsed, crashing into the undergrowth and stumbling over the rocky path. At the foot of the hill was Great Malvern town itself and it was there we found an Indian restaurant open for business, so we staggered in and sat there in our muddy boots, feasting on chicken jalfreizi. When 12am struck we were already dozing on the sofa at home, but woke enough to see the fireworks. Our evening was not exactly ground breaking in it's originality, but it was impromptu, which is always the best kind and very memorable.

I would like to be able to say that this New Year's Eve also passed by in a pissed blur, but sadly, I had to stay sober because Rob certainly didn't. Not usually a show off, Rob's abject reluctance to have a go at karaoke when not under the influence soon gave way to overt exhibitionism and he caterwauled as if his life depended on it, drunkenly pushing away anyone else who also wanted to indulge with an "Oi, I haven't finished yet". Maurice was the only person he permitted to join him and the two of them stood, with their arms round each other (Rob had to stand on a chair) with inebriated bonhomie and strangled a few Take That songs.

I'm very pleased to report we were absolutely packed and three of us behind the bar (but not Rob) worked constantly for about 4 hours. We had party games like pass the parcel, a raffle and a free buffet and, for the second time in a week I saw a lot of people I hadn't seen before, who turned out to live locally.

"Some potential new regular customers" I thought "Here's hoping".

Just before 12 we put on the radio to listen to the chimes of Big Ben, but the church clock opposite chimed as well so everyone trooped out to listen to the bells in the street. There were so many people in the pub that by the time the last people had plodded out the bells had finished so, like sheep, they just turned straight round and trailed back in again, wondering why they'd had to come out in the first place.

We all kissed and hugged and wished each other a happy new year. Do you know it was quite gratifying? I surveyed all these people who were having a good time and I thought, "They've chosen to spend their evening here with us. How good is that?" I ignored the fact we laid on free chilli and rice because I wanted to believe they were here to support us not fill their bellies with free food. And I really do think the free food was incidental and they would have come anyway, really I do.

In order to lift everyone's spirits in the post 12am lull we drew the raffle, the prize for which was a "minute behind the bar". There were two winners and each had to stand behind the pumps, one on the restaurant side and one on the bar side. The idea was to pull as many pints as possible in a minute and whatever they managed to pour they could keep. No spirits allowed, only pints. We'd carefully worked it out beforehand what the cost to us would be and we reckoned, the hilarity would more than make-up for any losses and we were right.

Everyone crowded round each bar to watch the mayhem. We rang a bell at the beginning and I kept an eye on the time. The crowd cheered each of the participants on and also offered advice to the poor individuals who were dashing around in a frenzy, miraculously avoiding slipping in the increasing beer slops,

The drink flowed well beyond two o'clock in the morning, but miraculously no one threw up. Not inside the pub at any rate. But there was plenty of clearing up to do. I couldn't face it at 3 o'clock in the morning after a long night of working hard, albeit making money. So I just took the cash drawer out of the till and put the whole thing in the safe, which is upstairs in our private quarters. Then I went back down in the bar to fetch Rob and managed to drag him up the stairs.

I am writing this as I sit amongst the debris in the downstairs bar listening to Rob moaning softly upstairs. I'd better go and check he's not in danger of choking on his own vomit should the need occur. Ho hum, the life of a landlady slash wife.

36. The Grumpy Man   January 2007

We've had a couple appearing on our doorstep at midday for a number of Saturdays now and they've always ordered a steak. We are reluctant to cook steaks at lunchtime, because in spite of all our efforts to increase it, the trade then is always bit slow and Rob doesn't want the expense of turning on the chargrill in case it isn't used. So we've developed a lunchtime menu, which concentrates more on snack food and bar meals and reserved the creative, more expensive foods for the highly populated evening trade. Nonetheless, for this elderly couple we make an exception.

On that first day they ordered two well-done rump steaks, with the added request the wife's steak was cooked so much it was burnt. That's the word she actually used 'burnt'. No matter that I explained the steak wouldn't be at it best, it's what she wanted and it's what we cooked for her. To her satisfaction it seemed.

Giles Coren, the restaurant critic for the Saturday Times, believes that asking a restaurant for steak is not a good illustration of what that restaurant is capable of. He reckons any damn fool chef worth his weight should be able to cook a steak correctly, and I agree with him. In spite of the fact we serve steak by the cow load, it doesn't really convey how good the rest of our food is, especially as, at the prices we were charging, we don't have much control over the quality of the steak to begin with. However, a good adage in business is 'always give the customers what they want' and if they order steak, no matter how blackened and burned that's what they'll get. Exactly what they ask for.

So Rob's been cremating two perfectly good pieces of prime Herefordshire steak for quite a few weeks now for this couple.

Except today. Their steaks were tough and dry apparently. How on earth they differed to those in previous weeks is anyone's guess. Rob chargrilled them in exactly the same way and for the same length of time he's done them before. I ask you, what did they expect? The old woman particularly wanted her steak burnt to a crisp. Any moisture in there had been sucked out a long time ago. The steaks were always so dry and brittle they were like pieces of wood on a plate. Tough and dry are the only remaining characteristics of well-done steak. We thought they liked them like that, but apparently, there's some subtle difference between charred remains you can eat and ones you can't, and we failed to spot it.

As they'd eaten most of the steak and the all the accompaniments, I did not offer to waive the bill. The departing frosty atmosphere told me they won't be back. I know I shouldn't take this too much to heart, but what singularly galls both Rob and myself is, as we discussed it later, in spite of giving them precisely what they'd asked for, by some vague and illogical benchmark we'd been judged and found wanting. Over a burnt bloody steak. You just know they're going to tell their friends, who in turn will tell their friends, that the steaks at the Bell are tough and dry. They'll omit to mention that that's what they asked for in the first place. Oh the injustice of it all.

Now this is depressing and incidents of this nature can certainly wear you down. It's definitely hard to brush off criticism like this, mainly because it's really unfounded and definitely unfair. But you just have to move on and Rob hasn't. He mentions this little episode several times a day and I know it bothers him.

Actually, for a couple of months now, when not in the kitchen he's preoccupied and monosyllabic. Grumpy is the default setting at the moment and he rarely laughs. When he does speak it's to seek constant reassurance he's doing ok. So, of course, my coping mechanism has swung into action and I'm trying hard to be his support, offering encouragement and consolation whenever it's required.

I like to think I'm not an out and out wuss. I don't flap my arms and squeal at spiders or have panic attacks if the lift I'm in stops between floors. I'm largely stoic and quiet in minor crises and just get on with it, whether it's a deep-cut finger, bubbling blood or my dog is racing away from me across a field and won't come back no matter how much I call the little bleeder.

The reason I'm telling you this, apart from to highlight how great I am, is to try and illustrate to you in someway that I'm one of life's copers. I tend to just get on with it whatever it is. I mean, you have to don't you? I had my son at 17. I was responsible for us as we both grew up. When there's a child involved it makes you dependable and reliable. That little boy was counting on me to feed him and clothe him. So it meant a full time job I had to keep, a roof over our heads I had to pay for and a rigid trip to Tesco's for the weekly shop, which, on reflection, was probably the worst bit.

All my life, it seems, I have had to be a support in one way or another, or at least, sort out things for myself. So, like a breath of fresh air, Rob breezed into my life when I was 36 and promised to take care of me. You cannot believe how relieved I was to hear that, so impressed and, yet, so pathetically grateful. Especially as, at the time, I'd just had my garden dug over by a landscaper who for some reason I can't quite remember, was unable to take away all the debris - the cut branches, the pulled weeds and the grass cuttings. There was a huge pile and I had neither the tools nor the strength to deal with it. I suppose, eventually, I'd have just paid someone to take it away, either that or I'd have left the waste to rot, sinking back into the soil for years and years probably until the big pile was gone.

Anyway, early on in our relationship Rob offered to deal with the garden rubbish. And I let him. It was at that point I fell in love. Probably a bit shallow of me, I know, but he was my bespectacled and balding knight in shining armour and because, most of my other boyfriends (and certainly the previous husband) had leant on me rather than the other way round, I thought Rob was brilliant. I realise there's a dichotomy here – on the one hand I was an independent, self reliant woman with a career and a mortgage and on the other I was a helpless, dependent female wanting a man to take care of me. But come on, people, isn't a working, single parent allowed a little respite sometimes?

Obviously, in the intervening years we have leant on each other, which is how a good relationship should be. I support him and he supports me. We're a team. It's him and me against the world (or so it seems sometimes).

So, this time it's my turn to be the rock. Rob is performing admirably in the kitchen, the stress, the heat and the vagaries of the customers do not appear to be fazing him at all while he's in there. After all, he's a bloody marvel. In our last business he taught himself to be a graphic designer using computer packages as if he was born to it and winning some big accounts on the back of it. And now he's a chef, and a really good one if the feedback is anything to go by.

Anyway, that's Rob. Just like Joe 90 (remember him?), with the glasses, but without Big Rat (the machine that transplanted the knowledge into the kid's brain). Instead Rob relies on his own resourcefulness, ingenuity and intelligence. He seems able to turn his hand to anything. I would suggest Rob's a polymath, but he may read this and get more bigheaded than usual. It's enough to say, I think, that he's very good at learning new things and putting them into practice.

But Rob isn't really coping it seems. My warm loving husband has disappeared and has been replaced, instead, by a bear with a constant sore head. It's very worrying. And he won't talk to me about it. I always feel a problem shared is one halved, but if I can't get him to talk about what's troubling him how can I help?

Does Rob hate being in the kitchen? Does he resent all the planning and preparation that goes into providing a full menu? Does he resent me for not having to deal with the same level of pressure? I really don't know, but I do know my man is hurting and I can't seem to ease the pain in any way.

Rob is doing a good job. We know that because the advance bookings are healthy, there's a steady trickle of walk-ins and the compliments from customers are flowing. So at least he's not worried because he thinks he's damaging the business. It's obviously something else, but what?

I have noticed the slightest criticism sends him off into a wave of depression. Regardless of how much good feedback he's receiving one tiny thing goes wrong and he wallows in the depths of despair as if it's a personal attack. His ego must be very fragile at the moment. So the burnt steak couple really has not helped the situation at all. It's not really their fault, I suppose, but I wish it hadn't happened.

37. The Pilot   January 2007

We had a really busy night in the pub tonight. We must be doing something right. I'm not quite sure what that is though. Rob's food seems to be enjoyed by all, perhaps that's it? We have a range of ales and lagers that are all selling well, perhaps that's it? I smile a lot and, when I'm not being surreptitiously rude to diners who arrive late, I'm can be quite warm and welcoming. Perhaps that's it? Perhaps the new décor has breathed some fresh air into an otherwise stale pub?

Though, I can't really believe that people are flocking to see our paint job and a few artfully arranged bits of fake fruit, but you never know. As they say, "there's nowt so queer as folk". There's no hiding the fact the pub has more atmosphere now, but I reckon that's because there are always people in it. Perhaps it's obvious we're making an effort and trying, as much as possible, to pay attention to detail.

We have three part-time bar tenders now and I've told all of them an important part of the job is to make customers feel relaxed and happy. They are given free rein to talk to people (when they're not serving others, obviously) and I've told them it's compulsory to chat with anyone who is in the pub on their own, with no-one to talk too. I've shown them how to bring these people into the general conversation or introduce them to other drinkers who they have something in common with. So, maybe our warm welcome is persuading people to come in more often and is bringing in new customers too?

You do have to be a bit careful though as I learnt to my cost this evening. One of our fairly new regulars is a chap in his early 50's who doesn't work and, as far as we can tell, has pots of money to splash around on hobbies such as flying helicopters. We were told (by him) that he used to be an airline pilot, which is quite impressive, but other locals have taken a bit of a dislike to him because they think he is arrogant and boastful and not telling the truth. I think it's probably just envy.

The Pilot also had an engineering company, which he sold for millions. I'm not sure why the other locals think he's lying because, unless he has an incredibly understanding bank manager, he's obviously wealthy enough not to have to work. And if that bit is true, it stands to reason the pilot story is true too.

I like the Pilot because he's intelligent, well read, experienced and has some good stories to share with us. He can also be quite controversial and, like a naughty schoolboy, thinks nothing of verbally prodding people to see what sort of response he'll get. The other day the Pilot came in to the pub, was served at the bar and wandered over to where I was sitting, talking to one of the retired farmers who frequent my bar on a regular basis. I think we were discussing the farmer's favourite subject, how much someone's land and house had sold for recently. Anyway, the Pilot pulled up a stool and joined us.

We all exchanged pleasantries, but the retired farmer was beginning to look uncomfortable as he was one of the ones who hadn't really taken to the Pilot. So I asked the retired farmer if he knew the Pilot and, when he said no, introduced them both. I was determined the retired farmer would get to see how witty, charming and interesting the Pilot could be, so I carried on talking about the farm that had sold recently simply because I knew the Pilot would have an opinion. Sure enough, he did and went on to tell us how much more money they would have got for the place if they'd only done this or that. We had quite a conversation going with the farmer joining in as if we were all old friends.

After about 20 minutes there was a short lull in the discussion so I turned to the Pilot and, in an attempt to prolong our three-way chat said,

"So, what have you been doing today? Anything exciting?"

"Yes," the Pilot replied:

"Oh right." I said with interest "What was that?"

"I have mostly…" and here the Pilot paused to give full impact to his words, "… been wanking"

He then picked up his pint and took a lazy, insouciant swig and waited to see what would happen.

There was a stunned silence for a few seconds and then I heard a chesty cackle. Turning to the retired farmer in surprise I saw he was laughing as he picked up his own pint to take a slurp. Smacking his lips in appreciation of the beer, the retired farmer said,

"That's one way to pass the time, I suppose"

I was quite shocked at how laid back the retired farmer was being about the whole thing, but wasn't sure how to move on from this. Instead the Pilot did it for me.

"Well, I went to have a look at a new Land Rover as well. Wouldn't mind buying one". And they were off into extremely familiar territory, discussing the pros and cons of different makes and models. I left them to it, but looked over at least an hour later to find them still deep in conversation.

So, I should have remembered the Pilot's talent for saying inappropriate things when, this evening I introduced him to a couple, I'd never seen before, who'd been sitting at the bar drinking for quite a while.

We were all chatting quite pleasantly for at least half an hour. I had left the bar for a break and was sitting next to the Pilot, who mentioned he'd been to Eton.

The lady of the couple thought this was very interesting and started asking questions about what it had been like. We were talking, quite innocently I thought, about the standards of education in state verses private schools when, like a fool, a thought occurred to me that came straight out of my mouth when I really should have kept it shut.

"Tell me, at Eton, did they have that tradition I've heard about where the young boys are, basically, the servants of the older ones?

"Yes they did and I think they still do. It's called Fagging", said the Pilot

"Oh yes, that's it. I remember. What are they supposed to do, run errands or something?"

"No. I'd say fagging is probably 50% slavery…" As before the Pilot paused and I knew at once this was a clear signal he was going to say something I wasn't going to approve of. I was right. He continued "…and 50% buggery".

(Rob has just read this bit over my shoulder and asked "is 50% buggery when you only put half of it in?" Of course, I slapped him and sent him on his way.)

So, there I was, yet another stunned silence, but this time the quiet was broken by a decidedly unappreciative nervous giggle from the lady at the bar. Her husband didn't look either impressed or happy. In a fit of panic and an attempt to defuse the situation I launched in with a full, throaty guffaw and a kind of Dick Emery style "oh you are awful" punch to the Pilot's shoulder.

The Pilot smirked, then relented, as he was too intelligent to let the embarrassment dominate and said,

"Well, something like that anyway. Although the Masters did discourage it. In fact all the traditions and rules at Eton are changing. A case of having too I'm afraid. Got to move with the times…."

Having veered off into much safer territory, I breathed a sigh of relief as the couple loosened up and began to chat again. The Pilot behaved himself thereafter and didn't throw any more verbal hand grenades into the conversation.

Most, in fact all, of our other customers are not as contentious as the Pilot, but perhaps this is because they all know each other and don't really have anything to prove. Instead they just take the piss and tell funny stories or, in some cases, spend an age talking about tractors or fertilizer. Actually, there are times when I could do with the Pilot to lob a conversational bombshell into their midst. Believe me, unless you happen to be a farmer or a terrorist, there's nothing interesting about fertiliser.

38. The Lorry Driver   January 2007

Well, what do you know? Our pub is in the local paper. Admittedly, the place is not mentioned by name only shown in a photo and I'll admit, also, that we are not included in a story that shows us off in the best light. The picture, in today's paper, is of a lorry driver walking down the main street of the village. You can see our pub sign in the background. The paper reports the lorry driver had been held in a French cell for a few days last week after customs officers found almost 400kg of Moroccan cannabis in his cargo.

At first I thought this was a great bit of publicity for us until I realised we were shown in the same picture as an alleged drug smuggler, so perhaps it's not so good. For a pub, not all PR is good PR and anything connected to drugs can sound the death knell. That and underage drinking.

The reason why the lorry driver is walking down the street outside our pub is because the guy actually lives in the village. And, boy, is everyone talking about it? I forget, sometimes, there are people who read every word in the local paper from cover to cover, including the adverts. So it was only a matter of minutes before a helpful customer bought the paper in to show us the story. The pub is now alive with the news and the speculation. Honestly, the villagers haven't had this much to talk about since Harold committed a murder in the church, years ago (now that is another story).

The villager was free to be photographed outside our pub, as the news report goes on to say, because he'd been released from his Gallic incarceration when a court accepted he was unaware of the illegal freight.

What a bloody lucky, lucky man he was. "I didn't know it was there, honest", must be the first protesting wails of all convicted drug smugglers and I'm sure all court officials across the world roll their eyes, give a deep sigh and settle down for the long haul, when ignorance is used as a defence. The court in this case must have been very surprised when the defendant actually turned out to be innocent. But I am wondering how on earth he managed to prove he was blameless?

How do you prove you had no prior knowledge of something? If I found a pair of woman's pants in my husband's coat pocket – how could he prove to me he didn't know they were there? The fact that I know him well enough to comprehend that a) he certainly wouldn't be foolish enough to leave evidence like that lying around, b) he has absolutely no opportunity to fool around at the moment and c) he really believes no woman (apart from me) would fancy him, can only lead me to the conclusion, straight away, that a) he's innocent and b) his friends are the most likely culprits. But this poor villager could not rely on an untarnished reputation because no one knew him. He was in a foreign country, away from home and separated from friends and family.

Yes, our villager was extremely lucky. The newspaper printed this comment from him "It was the most frightening thing that has ever happened to me. I was panicking and I haven't slept properly since I've been home". Poor man, what an ordeal he's been through. Apparently the villager was actually listed as missing by the UK police because he wasn't allowed to contact any family members to tell them where he was. Can you imagine the conversation if he had?

"Hello darling, how are you? Me? Well, I'm locked up in France for drug smuggling. Find a lawyer and send clean underpants".

So, as I said, the village is buzzing. The local newspaper was solemnly passed around the pub this evening whilst all drinkers read the story and studied the picture. It's thrilling that one of us has been thrust into the spotlight of minor celebrity, however we cannot revel in the vicarious fame because we don't have a bloody clue who the villager is. I've never seen him before; he's not been in the pub as far as I'm aware and none of the people who have lived here for years recognise him either.

One of our early customers this evening was Maurice who, I felt sure, would know this lorry driver because Maurice has grown up in the village and knows everyone. But as I tried to relate the tale whilst pulling him his first pint I could tell he wasn't listening. For a usually bright and chirpy character Maurice looked decidedly glum. I broke the habit of a lifetime and asked him if there was anything wrong.

"I've just lost the best part of 200 quid" he replied. This fact was weighing heavily upon him and he sucked in nearly a third of a pint in order to drown his sorrows.

"How on earth did you manage that?" I asked him when he came up for air.

He went on to tell me that it was his wife, Clare's, 50th birthday next week and, quite uncharacteristically for Maurice, he'd bought her a leather handbag to make up for the frying pan she was displeased to receive last birthday.

"It cost £187," he said staring gloomily into his pint. I realised he must be quite upset about spending so much money on what he would consider to be an unnecessary accessory and tried to cheer him up.

"Maurice, that's a great present. It doesn't matter about the price. It was really thoughtful of you. It's amazing you picked one out and actually bought it. I'm sure she'll love it".

"Oh I know she'll love it. I'll be getting blowjobs right up to her 51st birthday. It's well worth the money."

"So what's the problem then?"

"It's been destroyed."

I was astonished. I could not imagine in a month of Sundays under what circumstances anyone could destroy an expensive handbag.

"You didn't drive over it in the digger did you?"

"No" he said and went on to tell me what happened.

Apparently, Maurice owned an old and battered, lock up lorry container in which he stored tools and other blokey things (a bit like Rob's shed). I knew the sort of trailer he meant. Anyway, he thought it would be a great place to hide Clare's birthday present and had stuffed it in there a few weeks ago and promptly forgotten about it.

A week to go to the big day, and with forethought usually quite alien to Maurice, he'd decided to wrap the handbag up and had gone in the container to retrieve it. This was when he'd discovered that,

"The clasp's all rusted up and it's got big brown water marks all over it".

"Oh no" I cried, "That's terrible".

"That's not the worst of it." he said "I also found a nest of feckin' mice living it".

The thought that a family of mice had set up home in, what to them, must have seemed like the lap of luxury tickled me and I couldn't help laughing as I offered my condolences.

"Oh Maurice, I'm so sorry. What are you going to do?"

"I'll have to go and buy a-bloody-nother one, won't I?"

I tried my hardest to cheer him up but figured that if he was prepared to fork out another £187 he must be able to afford it, so it can't be all that bad. To take his mind off the pain in his wallet I turned again to the story of our infamous villager and showed Maurice the newspaper report and photo.

"Do you know him?" I asked

With a second pint under his belt, Maurice's happy disposition began to return and he gave it some thought.

"I reckon he looks like the bloke that lives up Foxhill, but I thought that guy worked at the fruit factory in town and wasn't a long-distance lorry driver." Maurice shrugged his shoulders, at a loss to shed any light on the identity of the wrongly accused.

This led to a common debate as to whether the newspaper report had mentioned the wrong village, but one customer pointed out that our pub sign was in the background of the photo, so it's definitely our village. It's a real mystery.

39. The Realist　　　　　February 2007

Not wishing to tempt fate or anything, but I do have a sneaking suspicion business is not too bad. During December, weeknights were busy in the bar every day whilst on Friday and Saturday evenings we were heaving and it happened too regularly to be a coincidence. The locals routinely packed themselves in to the public bar as if ours was the only place to go and en masse they greeted newcomers by name like the bunch of revellers in the TV Bar "Cheers" (they didn't always get the names right, but at least they tried).

We did more trade in the restaurant over December than we could truthfully handle, but we dealt with it, without having nervous breakdowns and this has enabled us to survive through the quiet January that followed. If February is as dormant as we've been led to believe it'll be, then we should have enough money to, just about, see us through.

Yes, December was really good to us. On New Year's Eve the pub was so absolutely jammed full with customers we were, as one of our regulars accurately observed, happily suffering from a bloated till. This meant I had no worries at all when only a few people appeared on New Year's Day. Yes, Rob did manage, despite a throbbing hangover and bleary eyes, to clean himself up and be sufficiently ready by 12pm on New Year's Day for anyone who wished to purchase a roast beef dinner from us. About 10 people took us up on the offer so it wasn't really worth it and on New Year's Day evening we had two drinkers the entire time we were open. Two people we'd never met before, in fact. Rob and I spent 99% of the evening sat by the fire in the Public Bar reading the books I'd given him for Christmas (good job I'd bought them really, wasn't it?)

So, it appears we have reached a sort of equilibrium, where all facets of the business are running along on an even keel, although I'm probably speaking too soon, something's bound to go wrong sooner or later and, no, contrary to what Rob says; I'm not being pessimistic, just realistic. There has been no part of our lives so far that have run that smoothly so I have every reason to believe there'll be a hiccup of some sort.

Last time I felt this smug was a few years ago when I was living in Great Malvern, a Victorian spa town built on the side of the Malvern Hills, a few miles away from where we live now in Herefordshire.

Great Malvern, for some reason, is packed full of old people – incomers who retire there. I don't know why because Malvern sharply rises and falls 500ft over its length. Many of its streets are so steep; running down them would constitute an extreme sport. Most journeys you make in Malvern feature a senior citizen out of puff at the side of the road. Brave or foolhardy, I don't know, but certainly admirable. In the last stage of life it's quite heartwarming these people retire to a place where extreme physical exertion is just part of the daily round and the price you pay for needing a pint of milk from the shop. Perhaps this forms the crux of why they move there, because it is often said of Great Malvern that people go there to die – and don't.

Famous for the "water cures" in the early 19th century, the Victorians loved Malvern, flocking there for holidays. Not content with building small, compact holiday homes they built magnificent, multi-roomed mansions many of which have now been converted into flats.

The conversions retained the Victorian facades and I bought what was essentially a very reasonably priced flat in a beautiful building. The best part about my flat was the living room that had a floor to ceiling bay window, which opened out onto the front garden – which was all mine. I loved it immensely.

However, the people upstairs, albeit a nice couple, had one serious failing, their excessive garden maintenance – in my garden. You know how it is, they offered once to mow my lawn, I presume because I was a) a single parent and b) out at work full time. I reckon they were also fed up with the mansion looking a bit untidy from the street. At first, I thought it was really nice of them to help me out, but before long they were cutting back branches, moving shrubs around and practically re-landscaping my whole bloody garden, which was a bit above and beyond the call of neighbourly duty.

I know some of you wouldn't see this as a problem, but it made me feel somewhat territorial. It was my garden and I actually liked it the way it was. I've always had a bit of a penchant for overgrown foliage. I don't mean it was full of weeds or anything, just that the hedges and some of the bushes were a bit exuberant and definitely not neat and orderly as obviously favoured by my upstairs neighbours. Admittedly, I should have said something, but it's really hard to be confrontational with people who think they are just being helpful. You can't really say to someone "Oi you! Stop moving my plants!" without sounding really stupid and not a little bit petty. I couldn't think of a tactful way of putting it, to get them to desist, so just watched, week after week, as the view from my big, bay window changed. Anyway, I thought my problems were over when they put their flat up for sale and subsequently sold it very quickly, to a middle-aged woman who was single.

It was at this point I felt smug. "New neighbours", I thought. "What could be nicer?" I should have known.

The first inkling I had that things were a little awry was when; a few weeks after she'd moved in, the new upstairs neighbour appeared at my front door clutching a can from which the label was missing. She appeared quite agitated and said,

"I think there's a problem"

"Oh really? Do you need a tin-opener?" I asked, pointing at the can

"No, no, something's wrong with my flat. Can I come in and check if yours is the same?"

And of course I let her in. It never occurred to me she was being less than sensible and could have battered me over the head at any point and stole my cat. She was my neighbour and at this point I was just concerned she was in genuine difficulty and may need my help.

She started muttering that it had all "gone magnetic". When I asked her to explain, she said that someone had switched "magnetism" on in her flat and she wanted to know if they'd done it to mine too. Obviously, it takes a slap in the face with a big, wet fish for me to realise things were not quite as they seem, because I genuinely thought she was joking and stood waiting for the punch line, whilst she roamed around my flat holding the can against any metal objects, like the fridge and the cooker. To her disgust she found my house was decidedly unmagnetic and left without so much as a thank you.

Subsequent visits bought questions about whether there was a switch in my house that controlled all her lights, because she found them switched off when she knew she'd left them on. Was I going into her flat and putting used jars of jam and marmite on her shelves? What had they done with the Houses of Parliament because the ones she'd just seen on the news were obviously not the real ones? And did I know if there was Helpline for people who couldn't find the right shoes because she was convinced they hid all the nice ones from her when she entered a shoe shop?

Before too long it became blatantly obvious that a bona fide nutter had moved in upstairs. About a year later and after increasingly eccentric behaviour, I had a visit from her daughter who told me her mother was a diagnosed paranoid schizophrenic and was becoming ill because she was refusing to take her medication.

"Absolutely brilliant" I thought to myself. "What on earth had I wished for? The re-designing of my garden was nothing compared to living beneath a mentally deranged woman".

So, as I said, contrary to what Rob thinks, I'm not being pessimistic about the buoyant state of the pub – just realistic. I know from bitter experience that just when you think everything is plain sailing, something comes along to upset your apple cart and put you up shit creek without a paddle. I know I'm mixing metaphors, or something, here, but I can't think of a better way of putting it.

40. The Older Chef   February 2007

Today we interviewed a chef and I think we're going to employ him. He's in his late forties and been a chef all his life so he certainly knows what to do. There is no doubt this chef can fulfil the role of the third wheel we were so desperate for at the beginning of this inadvisable adventure.

This guy came into our lives a few days ago. Approached us on a quiet night and asked if he could 'have a word'. We were as surprised as anyone when this random customer turned out to be a chef who lived in the village. He'd been working the other side of Hereford for the last couple of years and wanted a job closer to home.

Rob and I sat in front of the fireplace smoking the inevitable fag each and discussing the chef we'd just interviewed. For the first time in a long while Rob talked about how he was feeling.

It turns out, he hates being the cook (Rob refuses to be called a chef) and feels under enormous pressure to perform well, in order to keep our business afloat. He feels on a knife-edge, where one slip, one tiny mistake, could mean the end of our venture and the start of our journey towards bankruptcy. Rob reckons the daily grind of preparing food is killing him, especially as it all then gets eaten and he has to make more. He doesn't see that the food he cooks is an end product sold to customers for their enjoyment and to make money for us, he just sees that when it's gone it's a loss of all the hard work he's just put in.

Customers who eat Rob's food are, effectively consigning him to a daily grind of preparing more of the same. Day after day. And he takes no pleasure at all in the excellent feedback we're getting because one or two stupid comments from demanding customers (like the burnt steak woman) send him diving into the depths of despair, simply because they are a) not very constructive criticisms and b) could signal the end of our pub, if the complainants go off and moan, unjustifiably, to loads of people, who then choose to avoid our restaurant.

Rob feels we're at the mercy of crazy people who wouldn't know a good, value-for-money meal even if he shoved it in their faces. Something he feels tempted to do on a fairly regular basis. People are demanding, he says, and think we're only as good as the last meal they ate with us. The fact we're getting loads of repeat business is not encouraging him. He just sees it as more pressure. Oh dear. Poor lad. The problem, essentially, could be summed up in the last bit of our conversation,

"I always feel I'm out of my depth", he explained. "Have you never wondered why I don't change the menu much?"

I shook my head

"It's because I'm shit scared of moving away from the basics. I've learned to do the existing dishes inside out, but new stuff just makes me want to run a mile. It would feel like I was starting all over again."

"Weren't you just taking your time? Building up your confidence? ".

"Not really. I was just stuck with the comforting and the familiar and couldn't move on".

"But you're doing so well. People love your food."

"Some people do, but I do wonder sometimes if those are the sort of people who'd be impressed if I sprinkled some grated cheese over baked beans on toast".

"You're being too hard on yourself. And on our customers. You know people love what you cook for them".

"Do they? I don't think so".

"Of course they do. Our customers are mainly country folk. They're not going to part with cash for something they think is shit. Sometimes, it's hard enough getting them to part with money under normal circumstances, so the fact they pay willingly and we never or rarely get complaints must mean we're doing something good"

"I suppose. But I just felt like I'm not coping with it all that well"

"You look like you are to me"

"Well, I'm not coping at all. I feel like I'm sinking fast and it's only a matter of time before I make some stupid mistake".

"Perhaps you made a mistake going into the kitchen in the first place?"

"Are you saying I'm crap?"

"No, not at all. I'm just saying that many people would make the mistake of thinking they could pick up the reins of a job like that, but not many would do it as well as you have".

"Hmm. Well, I tried, but it's really difficult. I don't really like it"

"Why didn't you say something before?"

"What choice did I have?"

"We could have employed a chef for a start off".

"Look what happened when we did that before"

"We're thinking of doing the same thing again"

"I don't think it will be the same, this chef is older and more experienced".

"Well, there's no point in carrying on the kitchen if you don't like it"

"I know, but think of the cost"

"We should be able to do more covers with a more experienced chef, so he should pay for himself."

"Let's hope so. I'll make sure I keep an eye on his costs so the GP doesn't go down"

"Ok, let's talk to him again then. If he's happy with the terms then we can give him a job".

So we did and he was. Our new chef starts the Monday before Valentine's Day.

This evening, over a pint, I was telling one of our regular customers about the impending change in the kitchen.

"And it means we'll be able to do all the activities we planned, but never had time before"

"Mm. What did you say the chef guy's name was again?"

I told him. "Why? Do you know him?" I asked

"I think he's worked here before, about 10 years ago, when Stevie had the place"

"Did he? He's never mentioned it. How long was he the chef here for then?"

"About 4 years, I think, as long as Stevie was here".

"What was the food like?"

"I hate to tell you this but I only came in for a meal the once and never ate here again. It was crap. Undercooked and tasteless".

I was stunned. "Are you sure? Perhaps it was this chef's night off and someone else was doing the cooking?"

"Perhaps, but I'd keep a close eye on him if I were you".

"I'd intended to do that anyway"

"I hope it's alright then"

I didn't tell Rob about this conversation because I didn't want to worry him. Over the years this new chef has worked in all sorts of good establishments, some of which we know well. I've never heard a bad thing said about the food in any of them. In the light of Rob's declaration that he hates being the chef, I'm just going to keep quiet, but stay vigilante and make sure I test the new chef's food on an ongoing basis.

Business is going well, but I know it doesn't take much to kill trade completely and a horrible length of time after that to build it back up again. I will keep a watching brief.

I carried on serving pints for the evening, having a few pleasant conversations with some of the customers and desperately trying not to think about whether we were making a really big mistake employing this new chef.

A large group of about 6 or 7 people came in. They were visitors from a nearby village who meet up here regularly. One woman, about my age, wears the most amazing hats. Hats are not something people wear much and it's sad. I love them and wish we could return to the era where exquisite headgear was the norm. Anyway, today I plucked up the courage to tell this woman how great she looks,

"I must tell you, I love your hat"

"Oh that's kind of you to say so". She beamed at me.

"I've noticed your hats the last few weeks and always thought how good you look"

"Thank you very much"

"Yes. Your hats look lovely" I just wittered on. "I love hats. The only problem with wearing a hat though is when you take it off you get 'hat hair' you know what I mean? Flat and lifeless and cleaving to your head in the shape of a hat",

"I don't have that problem", she replied, lifting the front of her hat. "I don't have any hair."

And, indeed, she was as bald as a coot. Well that certainly took my mind off Rob and the new chef, I can tell you.

41. The Black Man   February 2007

I've learned to accept how gargantuanly dimwitted people can be at times and now bat away comments like "Is the Chilli con Carne vegetarian?" with a smile, or refrain from sarcasm when the customer's reply to my question "How would you like your steak?" is an indignant "I don't know, the chef should know that".

So, the quirky, misunderstandings and mistakes made by the general public who honour us by becoming customers are an amusing fact of this pub life and I quite enjoy them. It's all part of the fun. What I do find completely galling though, are those patrons who have an inflated sense of their own importance. They are the types, I feel, that would throw a tantrum if refused anything and are utterly convinced it is within their right to demand and receive anything no matter how unreasonable. I call them Pub Divas and thankfully we don't see many of them. However, on the odd occasion we do get them and last Saturday night was one of those times.

For most of the evening, we had more people squashed into our pub than I reckon live in the whole of the three counties around us. Then around 10pm the local amateur dramatic society, who'd finished their week long run of the latest production, bought all the cast, their families, friends and, it seemed their friends' neighbours and their families, to the pub for an end of show party. We were rammed. It was brilliant.

Quite why, the 100 or so unconnected to the am-dram society decided to visit us that night as well I really can't explain, but myself and the staff moved as a blur behind the bar and the locals had to stand so close they were practically drinking each other's pints. We were three deep at the bar and it was every man or woman for himself.

After about half an hour when we'd dealt with the worst of the rush and serving had become manageable again, a man approached me and said,

"I want to speak to the manager",

"I'm the owner", I replied with a smile. "What can I do for you?"

I beamed at him because this was a deeply attractive black guy. Tall, athletically built, wearing a polo-neck sweater and a long, expensive dark overcoat. "Very easy on the eye," I thought.

"I don't wish to talk here. Is there somewhere more private?" He asked

"Umm?" I looked round at the swarm of people still near the bar and said "Well not really, but we can step outside if you like" and I pointed to the front door.

Without waiting for me this guy turned to stride theatrically out of the building with his coat billowing like Darth Vader's cape. Outside he turned to me. I was still beaming at him in the hope everything was alright. Without further ado just said,

"I shall be making a complaint about your pub". Well that wiped the smile off my face, I can tell you.

"What? Why's that?" I replied, mentally running through a list of the evening's activities and couldn't come up with anything we'd done that would cause offence. Especially as the guy couldn't have been in the pub longer than half an hour.

"I believe I've been discriminated against. I was blatantly ignored at the bar and I know the reason I was deliberately not served is because I'm black"

Astounded, I sucked air like a goldfish out of water. Now I really have heard them all. I'll never,

ever complain again about the little foibles of all our other customers.

Now, can I say, on the record, I have no problem with black people whatsoever? It's true in this area there are not many of them, but there are one or two and they do use the pub fairly frequently. To me black people are just people and I welcome anyone into my pub with money to spend. I also have no problem with aristocrats, Hooray Henrys, gays, new age travellers, gypsies and chavs. I treat everyone the same - politely, friendly and with a view to making them feel welcome and relieving them of their cash.

I recovered sufficiently to say,

"I'm sorry you feel that way, but I can assure you that neither myself or my staff or indeed anyone in the village is racist. The reason you didn't get served quickly at the bar is because we are extraordinarily busy". Hadn't he noticed, the idiot?

But, no, that wasn't enough to change his mind. He went on to rant it was no less than he expected due to the fact he'd been dealing with this sort of behaviour all his life, rural villages and provincial backwaters are all the same, never see a black man from one day to the next and get all uptight when they do. I thought, "Wow, that's a really big chip on your shoulder."

I tried again to explain that in the pub or the village, no-one I knew was racist, we were just plain rushed off our feet and it was unfortunate he didn't get served quickly, but it was just one of those things. I even joked some of our regulars had to wait a long time as well and that really would be a grumble I'd be forced to listen to for the next few weeks. But no, nothing worked. The guy was adamant he'd been the victim of racial discrimination and he would still be putting in a complaint. So I just gave up,

"Whatever. If you must complain, then do so".

"So be it." He replied

"Tosser", I thought.

Back inside, I watched the black guy re-enter the pub, stride to the end of the bar and join the people he arrived with. He was talking indignantly and gesticulating wildly, obviously telling them what had occurred.

I know, I know. I handled the situation badly. I had kept my temper, but I hadn't poured oil on troubled waters and now we were facing an official complaint. To be fair, I wasn't sure to whom the guy could complain. The Police? Hereford Council? The Race Relations Board? And what could he say?

"The basis of my complaint is - I couldn't get served in a busy pub".

But still, I had my livelihood to think of. So in a last ditch attempt to salvage something from the situation I asked Rob to go and have a word with the guy to see if he could get him to change his mind. And after about 5 or 10 mins conversation, with the magic touch of a genius, Rob succeeded. The aggrieved chap shook Rob's hand and appeared finally to understand he hadn't been discriminated against. Rob asked him if he'd be pursing this matter any further and the man replied,

"No. I realise times are hard for the pub trade at the moment and I wouldn't wish to make it any worse." And that was the end of that.

Rob returned to the bar to tell me he'd calmed the guy down. I was very pleased.

"Funnily enough, the guy's name is Mark." Said Rob

"And?" I replied,

"Well when I heard that I told him we have another black guy who comes in here regularly called Mark. And we call him Darkie Markie".

"You didn't?" I was horrified.

"No, of course not, but wouldn't it be funny if I had," and Rob wandered off through the throng, tittering to himself.

Then today, three days after the incident, two police officers turned up at the pub to investigate a complaint of racial discrimination against us made by that black guy. What a complete and utter lying bastard.

Once we had indignantly explained to the police exactly what had happened they were satisfied no racial discrimination had actually taken place and said they would not be pursuing the case any further.

Rob asked if the officers had to report back to the complainant the outcome of this conversation,

"Yes, we will," confirmed the policewoman

Rob, throwing caution to the wind said, "Well, I don't give a toss about the fact he's black, but I do think he's a troublemaker, so you can tell him from me – 'You're Barred!' "

As I think I told you a little while ago, I knew, eventually, something would come along, to upset the apple cart. Now we're on the police radar.

42. The Devil's Brew   March 2007

I see plenty of people drinking serious amounts of alcohol in my pub and I never worry what damage these individuals are doing to themselves. I consider it to be none of my business. However, reading the paper this morning, whilst eating my breakfast (two boiled eggs from our very own chickens and two slices of toast from the - er- supermarket) I noticed yet another article about how much of a devil's brew alcohol is and how it warps the mind of our tender young things turning them into serial killers and nymphomaniacs (this is a slight exaggeration, but you get the idea).

I am, as you may imagine, particularly sensitive when it comes to issues affecting the pub industry. I have a sneaking suspicion the government thinks we are enjoying ourselves too much. Perhaps I'm just noticing more these days and singling out the licensed trade has been going on for years (or at least since 1997 anyway).

If we're not being targeted, how else do you explain trivial legislation that bans a customer calling a barmaid 'love'? I kid you not. Under proposed new equality laws being drawn up by the Government as we speak, extending a pleasantry of the sort just mentioned can open a can of worms and, unbelievably it's myself as a landlady, that would have to take the wrap. My customers who regularly refer to our busty barmaid as 'Sarah and the twins' (and you can imagine what the twins are) are skating on the thin ice that is sexual harassment.

Should Sarah be offended by this (and believe me she's not), complain to me about it and I fail to take appropriate action against the offending customer (which is not specified, so could conceivably be, public humiliation or, at the very least, withdrawal of a pint), then Sarah is well within her rights to sue me. It's breathtaking in its silliness, isn't it? In a recent landmark ruling the High Court was told, ' women should be protected by their bosses against 'regular objectionable conduct' by customers'.

The problem here is that 'regular objectionable conduct" by one person, is just seen as flirting by another. The crux of the matter, however, is if your barmaid is upset because some drunk made a lewd remark about the size of her tits or her nice bum, something which, evidently was meant as a compliment, then the employee has every right to complain to you, as the landlord. And you have to do something about it. In my opinion if this sort of thing easily offends a woman then she shouldn't be working in a pub.

Apparently, this new directive has happened in order to bring our law in line with EU ruling, but, like much of any new legislation, it's very woolly and not at all clear what is against the law and what is not. A disgruntled employee can complain to his or her boss after just two instances of so-called harassment and you're not allowed to tell them to get over themselves or provide them with a witty and cutting comeback. Surely the legislation needs to state somewhere "but keep some level of common sense and perspective about this, people".

Often, I wonder if this idiot Labour government of ours really knows what it's doing. The amount of minor legislation it's passing is breathtaking. Why ban fox hunting, for instance, when crime, the health service, unemployment, education, is all falling apart around our ears? Do the MPs assume, if they pass a few laws regarding the inconsequential trivia that make up our daily lives, we won't notice they don't have a clue how to solve the big things? It's the legislative equivalent of sleight of hand, I reckon, "quick, pass a law about squirrels and the public won't notice ASBOs aren't working".

Or do they think that we, left to our own devices, will descend into mischievous and troublesome behaviour, like naughty schoolchildren. The Government is acting like a particularly uptight head teacher.

Between May 1997 and June 2006 our Labour Government created 3,023 new offences for the statute books. Some of which are most insubstantial and plain daft.

It is now illegal to sell grey squirrels, impersonate a traffic warden or import potatoes from Poland. Why on earth can't you sell grey squirrels? Is there some lucrative money-making scheme involving these rodents I've overlooked? I thought the only thing you can do with a grey squirrel is eat it and why would you want to outlaw that? And Traffic Wardens? If you're actually a traffic warden all you can do is issue parking tickets. It's hardly as exciting as being a special agent or even a policeman, so why would you want to impersonate one? It's like posing as an Environmental Health Officer. Not much fun. So why do you need a law against impersonating a Traffic Warden I wonder? And I cannot even begin to understand what the Government has against Polish potatoes.

There's so much new criminal legislation the police service must be hard pressed to know whether you've committed a crime or not. Do they have a big fat book of criminal laws they have to take everywhere and flick through if someone looks even faintly suspicious?

The Government is not the only one to have lost all sense of perspective. A clairvoyant has been banned; by the Advertising Standards Agency from claiming she could cure everything from witchcraft to depression. The reason for the ban is because she can't prove it. Sister Charlotte claimed in her advertising leaflet to have a "100% success rate" stating. "I can find solutions for you in: love, relationships, marriage, job, business, family, money, finance, studies, exams, immigration."

She quantifies her achievements by saying 'I speak to my clients. They tell me I am effective at removing negative energies and relieving their physical, emotional and spiritual problems. If someone does not think the treatment works, I give them a refund."

However, because she could not provide any documentary evidence to prove she had "found solutions to people's problems in any areas of life," then the ASA ordered Sister Charlotte to stop claiming she could.

What happened to common sense here? I was going to say do people actually believe clairvoyants can contact Aunty Marge on 'the other side'? I thought psychic, crystal ball and Tarot cards were all taken with a pinch of salt like fairground attractions, but obviously not because I've read the ASA received 174 complaints in two years about clairvoyants. There really must be a lot of stupid people out there.

Presumably there's no such pressure to provide proof in America where TV evangelists claim daily they're in touch with God and Jesus and if you send them your cash, they'll put in a good word for you.

So, I'm reading the newspaper (remember) and I notice that in a few weeks time yet another law will be passed - the "Employment Equality (Age) Regulations

2006". Soon, it won't be a good idea to send an employee a birthday card that pokes fun of his or her age. So, to send a card like the one I saw the other day that said, "Old age is all in the mind. Unfortunately it's spread to the rest of your body too", unbelievably could be seen as victimisation or harassment. The recipient, if so inclined can potentially sue you, as the employer, for unlimited amounts of compensation. It brings you out in a cold sweat doesn't it? So, just to be on the safe side, avoid wit altogether, and just stick to the mild and inoffensive "happy birthday".

This, along with the Single Equality Bill, which will, in effect outlaw pub banter altogether, has the potential for such devastating consequences I'm beginning to think it's probably best to avoid employing people altogether.

So I decided to stop reading the newspaper, it's too bad for my mental health. I need to be creating happy thoughts, as my life is much too stressful to countenance anything else. I closed the last page of the paper and sat reflecting on the ways of the world, when Rob emerged from the bedroom. As he passed me by he gently farted and another flourish bubbled out before he left the room.

'Oi,' I said, in protest.

'Just spreading joy' he replied.

I wish they'd bring in a law banning copious farting in front of your wife.

43. The Strong Cider March 2007

We found out the other day who the mysterious Lorry Driver is in the local paper. He only lives up the road. His wife has been coming in the pub regularly with friends and family, so when she turned up for a meal with the lorry driver, I was very pleased because now I could tell customers it's me who's discovered the identity of the wrongly accused drug smuggler. Sadly, I cannot prove it by introducing him to anyone, because the lorry driver is not often around, as he spends a great deal of time on the road, mainly overseas. I hope he knows what he's missing.

Take the other day for example. I took delivery of a barrel of Old Rosie, which is now hooked up to a spare pump on the bar and pouring forth cloudy amber streams of 7.3% proof scrumpy cider. The locals round here love Old Rosie, especially as it's brewed by Weston's Cider, not far from us in Much Marcle (famous also as the home village of serial killer, Fred West, but the less said about that the better).

Needless to say, at around 7.3% this cider is very, very strong and only a whiff of it, I reckon, would be enough to make you light headed and giggly (well, that's how it effects me anyway). But as I said, our customers love it and we are selling quite a bit of the stuff.

It really is a bit of a challenge to ensure your trade remains buoyant and ideally, grows. I suppose the only way to do that is to make sure your customers are satisfied. Thank god we don't appear to have a problem at the moment. Business is good and we have a lot of both restaurant and bar customers. Whatever we are doing, we appear to be doing it right. You can't help worrying, though. Especially as I read in the trade paper the other day (the Morning Advertiser) an article that was entitled:

"Last chance Saloon for the Rural Pub"

The gist of the article was that the number of UK pubs is falling. Something like 3,000 have closed in the last 10 years – there's still around 58,600 left, so we don't have to worry too much at the moment – but, the article goes on to say, the heaviest losses are in rural pubs. That's not good, is it? Neither is the fact that those still open have seen beer and cider sales drop by 3.6% in the last year. It's probably because of cheap supermarket beer and the fact that Blair's government, like the puritans of yesteryear, seem to frown on this nation's predilection for enjoying a few good pints in your local pub, hiking up the beer tax and banning smoking inside. I must stop reading newspapers, it's far too depressing.

A little bit of good news is that, unbelievably, the value of pubs is up by at least 8% on last year. I think they mean Freehold ones, so what this means for the little man in the street who owns a lease, much like Rob and myself, and not the building itself, is anyone's guess. Still, the most important thing is to make sure our business stays buoyant and healthy.

Hence the reason for installing Old Rosie. 'Keep your customers happy' we thought and they'll keep our till ringing.

So, anyway, it was about 7.30 when Maurice entered the bar. As usual he was beaming and instantly lit up the place.

"Hello Maurice. How are you doing?"
"I'm doing fine thanks"
"Usual?"
"Aye"

It was at this point, as Maurice leant against the bar waiting for me to finish pulling his pint of Hancocks and shooting the breeze about the holes he'd dug that day, he noticed the Old Rosie pump. "Hang on a minute. You've got Old Rosie. How long that's been there?"

"Oh, only a couple of days or so. Why? Do you like it?"

"Last time I had Old Rosie, I walked home at the end of the night and woke the next morning to find my digger upside down in a ditch".

"Really?"

"Oh yes, apparently I started driving it round the yard at 12 o'clock at night. Crashed it in to one of the drain ditches I'd dug ages ago and left it there. Upside down. The wife was furious. And I don't remember a thing". He chuckled at the memory and I laughed with him.

"How many pints had you had?" I enquired

"Oo I dunno. 7 or 8 I reckon".

At that point Maurice's mate John came in and joined us at the bar

"John, John" said Maurice excitedly "They've got Old Rosie"

"Oh lovely. I'll have a pint of that then. Do you want one Mo?"

Maurice quickly downed the last third of his pint of bitter and, licking his lips, replied

"Oh yes. It'd be rude not to".

So I poured them both a pint of Old Rosie each and over the course of the next three hours or so poured them quite a few more. After about the third pint each I overheard them discussing how many pints of Old Rosie they could drink before falling down. Maurice reckoned he could handle 8, which was as a gauntlet thrown to John as they tried to drink as many as possible before the end of the evening.

After 5 pints each, they were fairly sedate, considering the alcohol content of the cider, but by the time they'd consumed 7 pints each they were guffawing loudly at everything they said and Maurice reckoned he really had drunk himself good looking. I must explain that in Maurice's head, the 'Beer Goggles' phenomenon works in reverse. After enough alcohol, Maurice thinks, not that ugly women are attractive, but that he's the most handsome man in the world. Something he doesn't think is true when he's sober.

The 8th pint pushed them over the edge into complete inebriation except that Maurice who was a considerably bigger chap than John was still making sense when he spoke.

I kept a close eye on the pair of them to ensure they didn't hurt either themselves or anyone else in the pub. But Maurice, a born entertainer, was literally sparkling with his wit and repartee. Mind you, by the 8th pint he was weaving about somewhat and I was afraid the big man was in danger of falling down.

By the time they were halfway down the 8th pint Maurice decided both of them had had enough. John was too far gone to protest and just slowly nodded his head, swaying in a vague semblance of someone who was only 15% with us. There must have been a glimmer of sobriety left in John's mind however, because Maurice was telling us, loudly, that John's party trick was accents. "Go on, John, do an Irish one"

And, astoundingly, John managed to speak in an Irish accent without making any sense whatsoever. It was really impressive. The man had real talent. He managed to incoherently drivel through a Geordie accent, a Liverpuddlian one and a Brummie one, all spot on and finely observed, but completely unintelligible. It was like listening to someone talking to you in a noisy nightclub. You can hear them speaking, but not actually tell what they're saying.

After they'd finished the 8th pint, Maurice respectfully bade us farewell and thanked me for putting Old Rosie on the bar. He then hooked arms with John and left the pub.

Through the bar window, Rob and I watched Maurice walking across the road towards home. He staggered a bit but managed to remain fairly upright. Unfortunately, he had, what Rob said looked like, his severely disabled brother hanging off his arm, falling into the road every now and then. Once they'd crossed, they stopped, in front of the church so John could throw up the whole of his 8 pints of Old Rosie in the gutter.

I feel I must stress here that Old Rosie, taken in extreme moderation, is a very nice drink. The fact that certain members of my clientele choose to view the opportunity to drink Old Rosie as a challenge to their manhood and drinking capacity in no way reflects on Weston's as a brewer or, indeed, myself as a landlady. Except, perhaps, I should have realised we were contravening one of the licensing laws. The one that states you are not allowed to serve someone who is drunk. Ah well. Too late now.

44. The Groceries April 2007

I read this in the local paper the other day. It was a letter to the editor, which said something to the effect of:

"Dear Editor
I am writing for no other reason than to use the stamp I had to buy as an excuse to visit the pub for a pint.
Yours sincerely
Jim

It appeared that the pub had opened a post office in one of it's back rooms and Jim was probably not the first customer who'd taken the opportunity to sample all that was on offer.

This is the one real advantage village pubs have over their town centre counterparts; they can provide the village with some of the facilities that have been lost. In our village alone we've lost at least three other pubs, the petrol station, the village shop, the butchers, the Post Office and those are just the ones I know about. I'm sure there have been plenty more businesses opened and closed in the last 400 years. The pub remains the last bastion of comfort and affinity (apart from the church of course, which has baggage attached). Luckily for us, though, we are now the only pub in the village.

It really is quite sad. Our village is changing, quite rapidly it seems. The services are disappearing and taking with them the palpable sense of community you get, bumping in to people you know well, in the grocer's or the baker's. However, much as I hate to condone the loss of our rural facilities, there's no denying the fact (and I do this shamefacedly, believe me) having no competition in the immediate area is of great economical advantage to us. No-where else for the punters to go you see.

In embracing rural living, though, it does make me sad the commercial centre of our village has died, but I'm sure this is a typical feature of country life these days. The shops close because the demand decreases. It's as simple as that. People can get cheaper beer/food/petrol etc., in town at the supermarket. It's easy and convenient. Mind you, some enterprising individuals have started a monthly Farmer's Market in our village hall and our post office is now a barber's, so that's something, at least.

A week ago, after much consideration (about 5 minutes, really) Rob and I decided, as we were intent on becoming the heart and, if our plans go to, er, plan, the soul of the village, it would be an oversight not to offer some of those extra amenities no longer available. So, we drew up a list of essential groceries - bread, milk, butter, cheese and, of course, chocolate and have been advertising those perishables for sale across the bar.

Of course, this is not as altruistic as it sounds, because we figure if customers have to come in for groceries they may very well stop for a pint or two anyway. Like the writer with the stamp, having to stop for a pint of milk is a great excuse to visit the pub.

To be honest, in a week I've only sold one pint of milk, so the demand is not great. I'm beginning to understand why the local shop went out of business.

The regular drinkers, also, didn't seem that impressed, when the 'Groceries for Sale' sign went up in the bar.

"Why are you selling stuff like that?" enquired Harold "Tesco's is only a couple of miles away".

"Harold, it's to offer a service to the locals. If they've forgotten a pint of milk or a loaf of bread then they can just pop in to the pub for it, rather than having to go all the way into town."

"Hmm. They should be better organised and get enough at the supermarket once a week like I do".

I sighed and was just about to argue when one of my regulars, came over to the Bar and said, "Ali, have you got a pint of milk I can have because I forgot to pick one up on the way home? It's for the baby so I can't leave it".

I beamed with surprise and pleasure, "Of course, you can. You know we're selling groceries now anyway".

"Yes I had noticed, that's a really good idea"

I cast a triumphant glance over to Harold, who, overhearing the exchange, looked very sheepish, as I left the bar to get milk from the kitchen. It was then I discovered, whilst I had copious amounts of milk in 2 litre containers, I'd failed to consider what I would decant this milk into to sell pints of it.

The only thing I could do was to pour milk in to a clean pint glass used for beer, cling film the top and send the customer on his way with that. Under the circumstances, I think that was quite appropriate, don't you? Because this one, single pint of milk in a beer glass is a perfect illustration of how our pub has the potential to go a long way toward replacing some of the services the village has lost. Let's hope we can sell a few more items now.

This is all very much in the spirit of Prince Charles' "Pub is the Hub' scheme, (something else I read about in the paper). Apparently, the scheme, which started in 2001, encourages rural pubs to diversify into other trades, which in turn, helps them to stay open.

The initiative was set up after the Countryside Agency found more than half all English villages no longer have a pub and seven out of ten have no local shop. Prince Charles is involved, presumably because the Princes Trust backs the scheme. I must say, there's always been something a bit 'country' about Prince Charles, don't you think?

I was quite inspired by this idea of the "Pub is the Hub" initiative, especially if they're throwing some free grant money around and did a bit of research on the Internet about it. Apparently, the scheme has helped hundreds of pubs in rural locations start additional services. Some 200 post offices have integrated into pubs, 80 convenience stores and 30 IT training centres. More imaginative, and successful, pub ventures have been a bakery, a pharmacy, a dry cleaning drop off and pick-up service, a library and, in one case, the relocation of village church services.

I found an engaging story about the launch in an old archived newspaper report. To launch the "Pub is the Hub" initiative Prince Charles visited the Craven Heifer Hotel in the village of Stainforth, North Yorkshire. I understand what they are trying to achieve but it does seem a little odd they choose to launch in a Hotel rather than a Pub, but there you go.

Anyway, this Hotel was chosen because the landlord and landlady had, the year before, set up a shop and a village Post Office in the Hotel itself. Prince Charles had a drink in the oak-panelled bar. A pint of Thwaites, which he declared was "very good", then he, according to the article, "exchanged jokes and Christmas greetings with the regulars at the bar before visiting the tiny shop and Post Office. The landlady told the Prince how they had set up the shop and the Post Office. The Prince Charles eventually bought a sticky toffee pudding, a Christmas stamp and a small Wensleydale cheese".

What I particularly like about this story is that Prince Charles paid for his purchases with "a £10 note he already had in his hand". Bless him. You can just imagine his aides deciding weeks beforehand it would be a nice common touch for Prince Charles to purchase foodstuffs himself as a PR exercise, then having to press a tenner in the Prince's hand at the last minute because presumably, like his mum, he doesn't carry cash. I'm also quite impressed the Prince knew what a sticky toffee pudding was, it's not the sort of dessert you think he gets to each much at Highgrove.

So, as a consequence of my investigations, I was very fired up about the 'Pub is the Hub' scheme. I had all sorts of ideas running round my head and Rob found me measuring up the bottom bar to see if it was big enough for a post office cum shop and off licence. My spirits have been dampened somewhat by Rob when he pointed out that diversifying would be a grand idea, but we don't really have the space. Also, I discovered, Prince Charles' initiative is concentrated on the North at the moment (how much focus do they need for chrissakes, its been 5 years!). There is no money available for Midlands based, go-getting, vaguely entrepreneurial publicans, like Rob and myself.

So, for the moment I will just have to settle for selling our small amount of essential groceries over the bar and see what happens.

45. The Customers April 2007

Incidentally, I must tell you, since we've employed a new chef in the kitchen (a breath of fresh air I can tell you), Rob's temper and general air of grumpiness has not improved in the slightest. He's still moody, monosyllabic and tetchy, withholds affection, and never pays me a compliment. I can't begin to understand what's wrong with him. Even the slightest incident sets him off.

Only the other day, a family in the restaurant was trying to persuade the Dad to be more adventurous in his choice of meal, saying things like, "Oh Dad, you always have steak pie and chips. Try something different for a change". The male of the family held fast against his wife and daughter, despite their entreaties.

"Leave me alone all of you. I'm quite happy with pie and chips thank you very much. If I have the same in each pub then I can tell which one has the best food can't I?"

There's a certain twisted, if unadventurous, logic in that I suppose and as I turned away to serve a newly arrived customer at the bar, I thought to myself that here was yet another example of odd customer behaviour to add to the plethora.

I had forgotten this encounter almost as soon as I'd turned away from the family. But not Rob. "What the bloody, buggery, bastard thing was that guy on?" he said.

It occurred to me that Rob's innate sense of humour and sanguinity seems to have abandoned him of late. This is fine if he spent his days working alone in a subterranean office pushing paper about and taking the occasional phone call, emerging only to blink into the light when it was time to go home. But, alas, Rob's current job is to serve members of the public who, I might add, quite frequently, albeit unknowingly, set out to push your level of tolerance to it's absolute screaming limit.

"Sorry?" I replied, perplexed "What are you talking about?"

"That guy", he pointed towards the Dad who'd earlier ordered steak pie, to the chagrin of his family.

"Didn't you hear him? He insisted on ordering steak pie"

"I heard him. But ordering food off our menu is not a capital offence. I actually think it's the point of our whole venture".

"Oh very funny." said Rob, his face twisted in disgust. "I meant that he only ordered the steak pie so he could use it to beat us with".

I had visions of the Dad smashing a steak pie over Rob's head, but I understood what he was trying to say.

"Don't be silly. I don't think that's what he was doing at all?"

"Oh don't you? Well you heard him. He said he always ordered steak pie everywhere he went so he could tell if the food was any good at all. Steak pie, I ask you. Why didn't he just enquire what the Chef's best dish was and try that? Any fool can make steak pie, it's as much of a benchmark of a chef's cooking as frying a steak".

I must tell you our heated exchange took place in a whisper in between the two bars, so no customers were actually aware of the disagreement. However, it's impossible to vent your anger in a whisper and all this just served to wind Rob up even more. He was not happy. I probably didn't help much by saying,

"Calm down will you, it's just not that important. You know what customers are like, I should have thought you'd have got used it all by now."

Rob just huffed and stomped off leaving me to answer the ring of the service bell in the kitchen and to deliver the plate of steaming hot steak pie to the errant customer, who, little did he know it, had been getting it with both barrels.

Rob's intolerance for customers is worse than mine. Granted he's not stupid enough to be blatantly rude to their faces like a short, bespectacled version of Basil Fawlty, but knowing him as well as I do, I can tell when he's thinking "Oh, we've got a right one here" even before his surreptitious, gentle sigh and the discrete heavenward roll of his eyes.

He does know that we're supposed to embrace the concept of "giving the customer what they want", but over the last few weeks especially, I sense that sometimes what Rob really thinks the customer wants is a good slap. To be fair to Rob, no matter how hard you try you cannot please all the customers all of the time and, it's a sad reality of the licensed trade you're going to upset someone sooner or later.

Although of course, Rob is of the opinion that he is more troubled by customers than they are by him. And that they give him grief in ways that are infinite in both number and variety.

According to Rob, it is quite obvious, in the eyes of some customers (mainly those from London, so he says) that the menu is merely a list of ingredients from which they can select with abandon, wantonly mixing and matching in order to create dishes that fulfil some passing fancy of what they'd like to eat at that moment in time.

So, they take the garlic mash from one dish, the chicken from another and the sauce from a third. But hold the ginger and the olives. And I'm a little bit allergic to onions, so can you leave the onions out? And is the chicken free range and all the ingredients from local sources? Apparently, they also believe Rob has every foodstuff known to man in the kitchen even if it doesn't constitute any of the dishes the chef has created.

Completely disregarding the fact the chef has carefully planned a delicate balance of flavours and textures, Rob says these people choose to believe they know better. He reckons their arrogance is breathtaking in it's audacity and he often wonders if this is something types like this only do when they are away from home visiting little pubs in the country or if they are quite prepared to play havoc with the menu when it's, say, Gordon Ramsey doing the cooking.

It's often the 'out-of-towners' too, who seem to think that apart from being a pub serving food and drink, Rob is also running a creche and is quite happy to entertain and control their boisterous, mischievous kids whilst their parents ignore them completely and just spend the afternoon getting pissed.

That's not all. Get him started and he'll tell you that vegetarians are another great headache.

"We're a country pub in the middle of Herefordshire," Says Rob "Nothing could shout 'Get your meat here' more than if we nailed a dead cow above the front door. So why then do vegetarians feel the need to huff and puff in disgust because only 25% of our menu is vegetarian? I would never visit a vegetarian restaurant and expect to be able to get a steak, so why do they demand more than three options of meat-free food from me? I'm sorely tempted to tell them that we do have a fourth option - crisps and nuts behind the bar or a fifth - they can just fuck off. I'm even tempted to point out to them that the steak was vegetarian when it was alive".

And on and on he goes. I work in the same pub and the customers don't bother me anywhere near as much…still, to take my mind off it all, I thought I would look into the origins of our pub. You never know, there maybe something useful to discover that could be used as a selling point to pull in the punters. There's no actual documentation to hand though, so I've been trawling the Internet looking for information.

I know the pub is old, dating back to at least the 1600's and that it was, at one stage, a coaching inn, but that's about all I've been able to find so far. What I have found though is some interesting and illuminating data about the origin of pubs in general. It seems from the moment they were invented the authorities have been trying to shut pubs down. The website of the Pub History Society (Oh how I wish they'd come up with a name that had 'Pish' as an acronym) says public houses in one form or another have been around since medieval times and, to this day, with a predictability bordering on the mundane, the authorities still view these places as hotbeds of dissension, drunkenness and disorder. In our ever-changing times, how ironically things have stayed the same.

Prior to the 18th century, public houses were alehouses, which sold beer, brewed on the premises, often by women known as alewives or brewsters. During the 18th and 19th centuries more pubs were built to meet demand in industrial and suburban areas, an increasing number of which were owned by breweries in order to sell their own beer.

Inevitably, the rise of the pubs meant more drunkenness, which led, as surely as night follows day, to more interference from the powers that be. In a twist on H L Mencken's definition of Puritanism, it seemed the establishment lived with the haunting fear that someone, somewhere may be hammered. As a way of controlling insobriety, which was endemic amongst sections of the working classes, the authorities wanted to close as many pubs as possible. It makes you wonder, given that we as a nation have continued to drink and get drunk for more than 800 years, why the establishment is still keen to dissuade us? They really are flogging a dead horse with that one.

Still, with my lovely husband gone and an angry, bitter one taking his place, it got me to thinking, perhaps the Government had it right and controlled pubs with an iron fist because they'd come to understand over the last 800 years the real adverse effects of a pub was not on the punters who get bladdered in them, but on the poor, overworked people who own them.

46. The Comedy Night April 2007

Tonight (and I hope you find this hard to believe) we had to break up a fight in the pub. I say 'we', but I mean me really. Yes, I ploughed into a tight ball of brawling males and emerged unscathed. Adrenaline was pumping round my body by the end and it was both frightening and exhilarating at the same time. I'm not suggesting we should have fights as a regular entertainment for our customers, but this one, at the end of the night, was certainly quite enjoyable. It made me feel decidedly badass I can tell you (for the uninitiated badass is slang for someone who has no fear, who is cool and tough. I know it's completely out of character for me, but I was worried about the furniture and standing on the sidelines pleading with them to 'be careful' was not really going to help on this occasion.).

It's a funny thing about violence (and here I'm talking about skirmishes between men rather than domestic violence) we all know it's not big or clever, but I think one of the main drawbacks is it's not pretty either. I don't know if you've ever witnessed a fight in a pub but the gents in question usually end up, spitting in anger with a red face and torn clothes where they've tried to grab hold of each other. As a display of masculinity, it really does leave a lot to be desired. Chaps, you look more like hot and sweaty six year olds after a particularly arduous tussle in the playground, especially if the fight messes up your hair. No, fighting is ugly and not because it contravenes any socially accepted male behaviour, but because, I reckon, it makes you look plain stupid, ungainly, uncoordinated and pretty much a loser.

Men are not used to fighting in the main, so when they do, they're not sure what to do with their limbs, can't control their tempers and end up grappling around on the floor, getting dirty and dishevelled, but not actually achieving anything. The only time, I think it's appropriate for any man to lie flat on his back on the ground is if he's in the throes of spontaneous passion (and by this I mean with a woman) or trying to fix the car. It'd be much neater (and there'd be more point), if one opponent stood still and let the other one hit him, but, of course, that's never going to happen.

Far better, would be if men, instead of fisticuffs, took to fencing, solving their disputes with a blunt foil. There's something a lot more skilled, dexterous and just plain sexy about a sword fight, don't you think?

Anyhow, here's what happened. For the last few weeks Rob and I have been planning a comedy evening. The start of our winning ideas to attract more people to the pub. Comedy nights are something we used to go to regularly in Worcester, when we had a life. Those events bring together all the best parts of going out for an evening. Drink, humour, entertainment, not needing to converse with whoever you're with and food (kebab and chips at the end of the night). Also, comedians are definitely funnier when you see them live. I don't know if it's because we're not watching the comics on the usually restrictive medium of television or it's the confined space and the intimate atmosphere that does it. Either way they're hilarious.

So when Rob proposed we had one of our own, in the pub, I immediately thought, 'Don't be daft; it'd be like trying to put on a Royal Variety Performance in the local Village Hall'. You get my drift? We have no room for a start and how do we find comedians? But Rob was way ahead of me on that one. He'd already discovered an agency to sort out the line-up and worked out we could fit around 70 people in the restaurant if we took the tables out. I was impressed. The guy had seriously thought about it. Best of all we could have 3 comedians and a compere for the piffling price of £300.

It sounded too good to be true and I said so, but Rob assured me if we put on a concerted effort to sell all the tickets beforehand then even if the comedians turned out to be crap and everyone was disappointed, we could make out it was just an experiment so we wouldn't have to give anyone their money back. Looking at this from as many angles as I could think of, I couldn't see any reasons why we shouldn't do it, especially as we could keep the public bar separate for the regulars and other customers who wanted to come in for a drink, but not attend the comedy night. So we chose a night of the week that was usually quiet (Tuesday), when we could afford to shut the restaurant and decided we would only charge £5 per person and throw in, for that price, free curry and rice.

The ticket price should cover the cost of the comedians plus the food and with 70 people in the pub on a usually quiet night; we should take quite a bit of money over the bar. So we went ahead and the tickets all sold out in less than a fortnight.

Then, with not much further ado than making vats of curry and piling all the tables in the barn out the back, we opened the doors for our comedy night guests.

The comedy was due to start at 8pm, but by about 7.25 all those who'd bought tickets had arrived. The restaurant side was packed and I was trying to encourage all participants to move down and take the many empty seats left in the front few rows. But no one would budge. They stuck close to the servery area as if scared it was going to be taken away. All too nervous to take seats close to the 'Stage' in case they got picked on.

I must just tell you the stage was in fact just an area close to the far back wall and next to a radiator. We arranged the chairs theatre-style all facing forward. In order to look more like a stage we set up a microphone in the middle and hung a red tablecloth on the wall as a backdrop with the word 'Smirkin' (which was the name we'd given to the comedy evening), cut out of bits of A4 photocopy paper and stuck on to the tablecloth with sprayable glue. It looked only slightly more professional than scenery for a school play, but at least we'd made the effort. Needless to say the first thing the opening comedian did was to take the piss out of it.

We also lost a couple that stormed out when I told them there was no meat-free option to the curry. They were quite upset and said they'd paid their £5 (a whole £5 I ask you). I pointed out to them the £5 was for the comedy and, in fact, the food was free and I'm sorry, but that's the way it is. They left in a huff. Vegetarians eh?

By 8pm all the comedians arrived and the evening kicked off to a flying start (after the derogatory comments about our home made backdrop of course). The compere, Ray, an Australian, was superb. In fact every comedian was a laugh a minute too, quite literally.

Strangely, a curious feature of comedy evenings is it's impossible to relate any of the jokes to anyone afterwards. I don't know why this is. Maybe because there's so much humour, the brain just mashes it all together and all you get is a warm and fuzzy feeling and none of the detail. The only thing I remember (and I don't think I've ever seen anything quite so wonderful) is the look on Maurice's face, when Rex Boyd, the headline act, broke through into the public bar where Maurice was drinking, (not wanting to attend the comedy night). Rex was wearing nothing but a pair of Speedos with two silver balls dangling off the front. Maurice very nearly choked on his pint.

The evening was an absolute roaring success. Not only was the laughing, long and loud, but 70 people descended on the curry buffet, stripping it bare. By about 11.45pm, most of the guests and all of the comedians had departed and I was just clearing up in the bar when I heard shouts and several large bangs coming from the garden. Someone rushed in from outside to tell me 'There's a fight'. I was horrified and rushed outside to see a cartoon cloud of punching arms and legs rolling along the side fence. There were actually about 6 people involved, all caught up together and moving as one mass up and down the wooden panels (it transpired afterwards, because one of the 6 was Rob, that 2 men were fighting and the other 4 were trying, unsuccessfully, to separate them).

It was at this point I saw red. How dare they fight in my pub? And with a loud 'Oi, what the bloody hell do you think you're doing". I ploughed into the midst and started grabbing arms and legs. Within a matter of seconds I heard one of the contenders shout, 'Ali's here. Stop, Stop" and the fighting just magically ceased. The four helpers removed themselves from the ball of men to leave the two protagonists each clutching a handful of the other's shirt and looking suitably ashamed. They were a couple of our regular customers who, whilst young, should have known better. I didn't actually grab each one by the ear, but the effect was the same as I marched them both through the pub, to the front door and kicked them out.

Both were pleading with me, saying sorry over and over again, but I ignored them and said I was seriously thinking of barring them, as I will not allow fighting. I told them to come back tomorrow to apologise and talk to me about it. Suitably chastised each man sloped off in a different direction, head hung in humiliation.

Now, as I said at the beginning, fighting is not pretty and those involved always look really stupid, as I think I've shown here. I haven't yet found out what those guys were fighting about and I don't really care. They obviously had some beef with each other, but instead of dealing with it in a calm and rational matter, they resorted to punches and making themselves look complete and utter fools. All this, however, did have the pleasing effect of making me look really good. Something that doesn't happen very often, eh?

47. The News Report   April 2007

Surprise, surprise – we now know that the smoking ban will come in to effect on July 1. I think I've mentioned to you before that I'm quite looking forward to it and, indeed, this warm weather, with everyone choosing to smoke outside instead of in the bar, has given me a taste for how ash free and clean my pub will be. So I, for one, can't wait.

What is worrying, however, is that we asked for our smoking shelter to be completed by Easter, which was a week ago. Is it finished? Is it hell. The workmen, like workmen probably the country over, appear for a couple of days then disappear completely for a few more. Where do they go and why? Surely it would make more sense to finish one job before disappearing off on another, which is what, I assume, they are doing?

It'd help enormously if they achieved a little more whilst they were actually here. Last week I watched them install the actual smoking shelter itself. Now this was a real event and the only building work Rob and I have felt compelled to be present for. It was a bloody good job we were there.

Previously a square patio of Cotswold stone slabs had been laid on which the shelter would rest. So far so good. Then a wooden, structure arrived which was the shelter. It was magnificent. Made of wood, with 6 sides, glassless windows on two of the sides and a doorway on a third. It had a roof rising to a point in the middle, which had a ball on the top of it. Much more like a garden house, in fact, than a ropey old smoking shelter.

It was quite substantial and particularly heavy, requiring about 5 builders to lift it into position. Which they did, with much grunting and swearing, shifting it this way and that to find the optimum place for the doorway. Eventually we all stood back to admire it and noticed straightaway, it was far too small. It looked more like a sentry box than a smoking shelter designed for 6 to 8 people.

"Er" said Rob "Are you sure that's right? It doesn't look big enough."

The chief builder, or whatever he's called, admitted it wasn't and, in fact, our shelter had been sent, by mistake, to another pub and we'd received their's.

"We thought we'd give it a go anyway and see what it looked like once we'd got it in place". Reasoned the chief builder. "It doesn't look too bad".

"Doesn't look too bad?" Said Rob "It looks stupid."

I think the chief builder realised we had caught him out trying to fob us off so, after little argument, the chief builder agreed to take it away and replace it with the one we are supposed to have. We're still waiting. Easter, as I said, has come and gone and our smoking solution remains unfinished. Humph.

Encouragingly though, the courtyard between the smoking shelter and the pub looks lovely, and I've dressed it with a few hostas in pots and a garden table or two. So that's where we were, this evening, 6 or 7 of us standing there, trying it out whilst idlely smoking a fag and shooting the breeze about nothing in particular, just enjoying the half decent surroundings and the sunshine.

The weather in England is a weird and wonderful thing, don't you think? One minute it can be raining and cold and the next warm and sunny. And that's just in the space of one day. At the moment it's really hot and it's only April. This means we're either going to have a fantastic summer weatherwise or this is the summer - one month of sunshine and that's our lot.

The only problem with good weather at the wrong time of year is that I never know what to wear. I'm like one of those old people you see who always appear to be wearing layers of clothing when it's really hot. Do they feel the cold I wonder or are they sticking stoically to a deeply held belief that because it's still spring they cannot possibly wear summer clothes no matter how baking it is?

I must be the same, or a bit slow on the uptake because it takes me a while to realise I should be wearing less clothing. It's almost like I subconsciously can't believe it's warm and therefore choose to ignore it. As a consequence I'm still wearing winter woolies whilst everyone is in T-shirts or short sleeves. In my defence, I do get cold very easily, so I always assume I'm going to be cold and dress accordingly, - until I realise I'm far too hot. It's silly really, but I also get caught out the other way round too.

In the past, when we had a life, Rob and I went to Thailand a couple of times. In December. At that time of year in the Far East the weather can reach anything up to 42 degrees C. Very hot and incredibly sweaty. So, having left the country to come home, you are always wearing completely inappropriate clothing when you get off the plane in freezing Britain. At least I am. Everyone else acquires armloads of padded jackets, woolly jumpers and thick socks that seem to materialise from nowhere whilst they're on the 'plane. I've watched and there is no way they are carrying this gear with them when they board. So where does it come from and why am I the only person standing shivering at the English luggage bay in thin cotton trousers and sandals?

For this month, at least, I've hit it just about right, I think, with my usual black trousers and a shirt instead a polo neck sweater. And a cardi or a coat handy for when I do get cold, as I inevitably will. Especially as the evening regulars have taken to standing outside in the almost finished refurbished courtyard and, of course, I've been joining them when I can. If the weather this summer is half as good as this then the courtyard is going to be a godsend.

So there we were, enjoying a convivial cigarette when, apropos of nothing, Nick, a farmer said, "Did you see that news report in the local paper today about an abandoned tractor?" We all agreed we hadn't and I went off to fetch the newspaper from the bar. I returned a few minutes later with the journal having found the article Nick had been talking about and placed it on the garden table. We all poured over it.

The gist of the article was that the police were appealing for the owner of an old Massey Ferguson tractor to come forward. The farm machinery had been found abandoned in a ditch on the road between our village and Ledbury in the early hours of last Saturday morning.

The vehicle's engine was still running and there was no sign of anyone in or nearby. There were no registration plates and the police have been unable to identify its owner from the chassis number and there have been no reports of a tractor stolen.

"That's our tractor," admitted Nick

"Really?" I said. "What was it doing in a ditch outside Ledbury?"

"Jason was driving it" Nick continued

The light of comprehension shone on all present and we nodded. We all knew Jason. He is Nick's cousin and 17 years old. Jason is a farm labourer and as such was able to drive a tractor on the public highway because he's passed his driving test. Jason had figured that, as he was unable to afford a car of his own and his dad had an old tractor that was not used on the farm anymore, he might as well use the tractor as his form of transport. Like many people in the country, resourceful, Jason saw a purpose for a redundant machine and put it to good use. I often saw him rumbling passed the pub perched atop his tractor, on his way out for the evening. It's also not the first time I've seen one or two other farmers use their tractors as transport. One old chap I know used to fetch his daily paper on his.

So, as we nodded in understanding, one of our number asked,

"Drunk was he?"

"Oh yes", replied Nick "As a skunk"

Jason had crashed his tractor on the way home from the pub. Now before you all shout in disapproval, I know Jason is only 17, although he does look a lot older, and, therefore, he is not allowed alcohol in our pub. Jason, who is amicable in the extreme, knows and accepts this, so does his drinking in Ledbury instead (Ledbury is our closest town and, whilst extremely picturesque, does have a chemist with a big sign in the window that says "Chlamydia tests while you wait". I'll leave you to draw your own conclusions).

I'm not about to comment on the whys and wherefores of those establishments in Ledbury who are willing to serve Jason alcohol, I'm just telling you this story. So, Jason got drunk in town, tried to drive home, crashed his tractor in a ditch and, because he, like all of us, assumed you're not allowed to be drunk in charge of a farm vehicle, just legged it.

"What's he going to do?" Someone asked

"What can he do? He's a stupid prick for losing his only form of transport. There's no way we can get the tractor back without landing him in it".

Nick said Jason's dad was very annoyed his son was driving under the influence and more than a bit miffed he'd lost the tractor as well. We all laughed and someone said Jason should use a horse and cart or a skateboard instead because, whilst you can be fined for being drunk in charge of said transport, you can't actually lose your driving licence.

After a while we stubbed out our fags and trooped back in away from the brilliant sunshine to the gloom of the pub. The men were in their shirtsleeves and because it was really hot and I still hadn't caught up with the weather, I was wearing a heavy coat. Still, as I'd been told before, it improved my figure no end.

48. The Surprise   May 2007

I was right to be 'realistic'. I knew something would go wrong eventually. It was all too good to be true and now, today, we've probably destroyed our reputation forever.

The day started off well. The sun was shining. We had a busy lunchtime ahead of us, with a party of 16 booked and I was feeling chirpy. Annoyingly so, I imagine, because it was Sunday, the day after a particularly liquid Saturday night and Rob, amongst others, was nursing a hangover and wincing every time I spoke to him. No matter though, "What could go wrong?" I thought. What indeed.

A party of 16 was booked in for 12.30 by which time only 6 had turned up. I may have mentioned before, but late arrivals cause us no end of trouble. Being only a small pub with few staff, a party this large means we are unable to serve anyone else whilst we feed them, so I'd allowed an hour in which to take their order, sit them down and cook and deliver their meals. Consequently, we had to have them eating by 1.15 at the latest in order to then deal with the bookings I'd made for 1.30, 1.45 and 2pm.

It's such a balancing act because, not only are we trying to please those who have booked, I also attempt to fit in, what I call, Walk-ins, customers who have popped in on the off-chance of getting a table. Sunday is a day most suited to making a lot of money at lunchtime because many people want to eat and it's not that difficult serving roast dinners as most of the cooking has been done beforehand. So I try to pack in as many as I can, but the latecomers in the party of 16 were seriously messing up my plans.

By 1pm as another six had turned up, the 12 decided not to wait for the remaining 4, so ordered their meals, then trooped out into the garden, where they had demanded to eat, rather than in the restaurant. By this time, I was more than a little miffed, as I'd had to turn away 7 other diners in the half an hour we'd been pissing about.

Anyway, lunchtime was well underway, and around 1.40 I happened to be behind the bar serving a round of drinks when I noticed a man with a small child tapping his fingers on the bar (the man not the child). I finished serving my existing customer and turned to the man with a pleasant, albeit less chirpy than first thing that morning, look on my face. I asked him if I could help and he told me he was ready to order now.

This was flummoxing because at no point had I sat this man down at a table so I knew he was neither a book-in nor a walk-in. And besides, the kitchen was flat out. I wouldn't be able to take any more orders for a while and had managed the situation in the restaurant accordingly. Or so I thought. So I said 'pardon' and the man said again, getting a bit impatient I thought, that he wanted to order food now.

"Have you booked?" I asked

"Yes I have. Our table was booked under the name Harrison". Ah, a light bulb switched on in my head. This man was one of the party of 16 booked in at 12.30. I told him I couldn't take his order at the moment and tried, as pleasantly as possible to explain we had other diners to serve first.

"I had a booking at 12.30. So I should be served now," said the man. I tried to patiently explain that he was an hour and a half late, but I'd try to get to him as soon as I could.

"You can't do that. We have children with us and they need to eat now."

I told him I was sorry, but there was still going to be a wait of half an hour or so. The man went alarmingly red in the face and blustered at me. As if that was going to make any difference. No amount of raving was going to persuade me to allow him to jump the queue. Eventually he gave up and stomped off towards the garden with the parting words,

"Oh you can stuff your dinner. I'm not going to be treated like this. We won't be eating."

He was affronted. I could tell and I was apoplectic at his arrogance and complete inconsideration. However, he didn't know that, because whilst he was raging at me, I kept my calm and smiled. This man was a bully who thought the way he behaved would bulldoze me in to agreeing to his demands. I didn't care, though. I am providing a service but that doesn't mean I have to acquiesce to unreasonable demands. I'm not a slave.

Now please don't get upset on this guy's behalf. I know you're all used to an abundance of chain pubs that are open all day and have millions of staff to throw at the enterprise so you can get a meal at the drop of a hat at any time of the night or day. But that doesn't mean all pubs are like that. Some, like mine, have small capacity and you just have to wait. I'm sorry, but there it is.

So, by 2.30, with only a couple of tables left in the restaurant, I was riding high on my, albeit pointless victory, when one of the last diners came over to the bar where I was standing and said the words that caused shivers to run up and down my spine and the small hairs on the back of my neck to raise in alarm.

"I'm afraid there is dog muck at the bottom of your restaurant and my daughter has just stood in it". OH. MY.GOD.

The icy horror of failure stared me in the face. Rejection, ostracism, empty restaurant, empty pub, debts and bankruptcy flashed before my eyes. In a moment I dropped from feeling quite buoyant and happy down to the depths of despair. I did the only thing I could think of under the circumstances. I babbled apologies and in a hot sweat and with a burning red face I went to clear up the mess, pausing briefly to sob at Rob who was helping out in the kitchen. I tearfully pleaded with him to go and speak to the customer as I was little more than useless unable to get pass the sheer enormity of the problem. All I could think was "Poo! Poo!" flashing like an alarm in my mind. I was a wreck I can tell you.

Rob, bless him, took complete control talking calmly to the customer, waiving his bill completely and promising to shoot our dog, who we surmised was the culprit, at the earliest possible opportunity.

The only saving grace of this whole debacle was that the customer had been extremely discreet about his complaints. I dread to think what would have happened if it had been the hostile and offensive latecomer from the party of 16 who'd found our dog's little surprise. We really would have been in a world of shit then I can tell you.

Whilst the unfortunate customer didn't go away exactly happy, Rob did manage to placate him and, as the customer said, he had been quite enjoying himself up to that point and the food was lovely. I know he won't be back though, would you? I'm paranoid about what is being said about us out there. I'm also checking for poo, morning, noon and night. I am the poo monitor.

I reckon this whole running a pub malarkey is the same process as learning to drive. To start off, the prospect of negotiating your small car around roads and roundabouts brings you out in a cold sweat. Other cars on the road are monsters all out to get you and you never know which gear you're in so keep glancing down at the gear stick to check. This means taking your eye off the road for a second, causing the car to swerve alarmingly and the instructor to frantically pump his foot up and down on the dual-control brake as if his life depended on it. Which, in my case, it often did.

But pass your driving test and before long you are driving at 60 miles an hour as soon as you let the brake off, lurching into the traffic at roundabouts with a certain casual indifference and overtaking on the motorway as if it were a national sport you think you have a talent for. For something so terrifying at the beginning it's quite amazing how quickly you instinctively drive without thinking. It's like not having to remember to breathe.

Running a pub is not an intuitive occupation, in spite of the fact I have spent a lifetime in them and probably absorbed some knowledge as if through osmosis. Nope, whilst I am now a fair way down the road, there is still a long way to go. I still don't know, for instance, whether the gas cylinders, of which there are two, are connected to the right pump. It makes a difference you see because one controls the soft drinks pump, lemonade, cola and the like, and the other controls the ale, the lagers, ciders and things. There's different gas in each and I'm not really sure which is which when they need changing. I also haven't asked the question as to what would happen if the wrong gas cylinder were attached. At best the liquid would fail to come up the pipe or at worse I could blow the place up. Who knows?

What I do know though is, whilst it's an extremely hard slog and takes a long time to build up a good reputation it's easy, in less than a blink of an eye, to lose it. So, to torture the driving analogy even further, I feel now we have crashed and are off the road, upside down in a ditch. Ho Hum.

## 49. The Husband					May 2007

I was serving behind the bar alone this lunchtime. Rob was off somewhere pottering. It was about 1.30pm and we'd had a few people in for food, but not many and there were four or five people left drinking in the bar, mainly farmers taking a break. It was a rainy day, which didn't help. After a glorious start in April, full of promise for a hot June, July and August, it seems we are now destined for rain, rain and more rain. This summer's not shaping up at all is it?

Anyway, a bloke I knew to be a farm labourer, had just left the pub and soon after there was a squeal of tyres as a car screamed to a halt outside the front door. The few drinkers in the bar, turned their heads to the window to see a man, whom I didn't recognise, propel himself out of the driver's seat and run headlong into the pub, leaving the engine idling.

This man threw open the door to the bar, causing it to bang loudly on the table behind and without saying hello, introducing himself, asking politely for a pint or indeed any of the opening pleasantries you normally associate with people entering a licensed premises, demanded, with quite a lot of agitation,

"Where's Mickey? Where's Mickey?" The drinkers in the bar shook their heads, mostly to denote they didn't know, but also in shock and surprise.

In frustration the angry man turned to me and said, "Do you know where Mickey is?" He was glaring at me menacingly so, panicking, I said, without thinking, "He's gone, you just missed him". For Mickey was, in fact the farm labourer who'd just left. This unknown man, turned abruptly, fled the pub and ran back to his car, climbed in and raced off down the road.

Those of us left behind looked at each other in bewilderment and I asked, "Who was that?" "The Doctor's Husband" said one of the customers. Curious, we all crowded round the window to see where the car had gone, but the bend of the road made it impossible to see further than two houses down and, by that time, there was no sign of anyone. "I wonder what the problem is?" I speculated out loud. The remaining customers said they didn't have a clue.

Later that evening we heard what happened. As you can expect in a village, I was told this tale, from a Farmer, who heard it from his wife, who'd heard it from her friend who was the wife of one of the witnesses. So it must be true then.

Apparently, after the Doctor's husband drove away from the pub, he spotted the farm labourer further down the street. The farm labourer must have heard the car approaching at speed and turned round to see the vehicle being driven directly towards him. In horror, farm labourer sprang to one side, misjudging his landing and tumbling over in his haste. I can imagine he crouched there with his arms over his head, steeling himself for the impact.

Luckily the car stopped short so Farm Labourer immediately picked himself up off the floor and, not seeming shaken at all, ran towards the Doctor's husband, who was half out of the car, shouting abuse across the bonnet. Without saying a word, Farm Labourer just punched the Doctor's husband, full in the face, who dropped like a sack of spuds. Farm Labourer then just calmly walked away and went home.

The Doctor's husband wasn't badly hurt because, when he'd finished flapping around on the ground like a landed carp, managed to get his mobile phone out of his pocket and call the police.

The Bowls boys, playing on the green at the end of the village, were the only ones who'd witnessed the whole event, their disembodied heads peering over the end wall in amazement. So when the police duly arrived the Bowls team were the only ones able to give statements.

It transpired that Farm Labourer had been gossiping about the Doctor's husband's son who had been sacked from his job. Somehow, the Doctor's husband had got to hear about the tittle-tattle, it's not hard to imagine how, and was mightily upset about what had been said. Without further ado the Doctor's husband decided to take matters in to his own hands and, reasoning that it was an appropriate response to the crime of gossip mongering, tried to run over the farm labourer. You couldn't make this up any better could you?

I understand the Doctor's husband dropped the charge of assault against the Farm Labourer when it was pointed out to him that it really was a worse offence to try and run someone down in your car. But I don't know the legalities of all of this. I do know, however, that neither of them was charged this afternoon.

Needless to say, the pub is alive with the story and every time I walk passed a huddled group I can hear them whispering away. No real harm's being done because all they are doing is talking and I know that as soon as then next thing to talk about comes along they'll have forgotten this one.

It was just the same when Harold committed murder in the church. A squirrel had been trapped in there for some time, resisting all attempts to remove it and keep it alive. It was causing quite considerable damage in its terror and frustration and the villagers were at a complete loss as to what to do about it. So, Harold, with great presence of mind, I thought, just got his gun and shot it. Cold, stone dead with the first shot. I think that's really impressive, because, no matter how easy they make it look on the TV, to shoot a moving target cleanly with your first shot is the sign of a crack marksman (either that or Harold's had a lot of practice at shooting squirrels). Anyway, because something had been killed in there, the church had to be re-consecrated by the bishop. Or so I've been told because I wasn't living around the village when this incident took place. I'm just repeating gossip from years ago. However, I don't know if this tale is true. I haven't been able to confirm it because the vicar just tuts when you mention it.

But that's by the by. I was telling you about the Doctor's husband, an incident that has set me off thinking. I have noticed on numerous occasions in the pub, and I might add in my previous life, that some women feel the need to be their husband's keeper.

You know what I mean. You've all seen that man outside having a sneaky puff on his mate's cigarette when his wife's not looking. Why does that man not just light up with wanton abandon and hang the consequences? Is he trying to avoid being caught in order to save himself from a world of grief? I cannot believe either the wife or her husband is deceived, she would know he's having a crafty smoke by the smell on his breath if nothing else and he surely knows he's not really getting away with it. Are they, in reality, complicit in their mutual deception?

Many wives treat their husbands like naughty school kids all the time. During my childhood I often watched my mother dole out money to my dad as if she were giving him pocket money. In fact, that's exactly what she was doing. Giving him an allowance per week in order that he didn't spend the electricity money on high living - like a packet of cigarettes or an extra pint. My father was never one to be extravagant so I do not understand the reasoning behind this parsimony. Unless, of course, it was really all about control.

Then there's the mother of a friend of ours who does not allow her husband, under any circumstances, to drink more than two pints of real ale when he's in the pub (I'm not sure if this only applies when he's accompanied by his wife). What does she think he's going to do if he has that evil third pint? He's 67 for chrissakes. Drop his trousers and moon the punters? Cop off with the barmaid?

I do not understand this need some women have to mother and control their spouses. Do they think there's an inner child in their men folk that requires vigilant policing at all times and a telling off when they do something wrong? Hang on, though, after the incident with the Doctor's Husband I'm beginning understand the wisdom of keeping your other half on a short leash.

No, that's silly. If Rob makes a fool of himself it's only him that looks bad, not me and he's perfectly capable of accepting the consequences of such actions. He is the sort of bloke who knows his own mind and doesn't need me to tell him what to do. Whatever Rob did, I'd just tell him he was a big, stupid idiot and not worry at all how that reflects on me because he's never concerned my behaviour will reflect on him. Which is bloody lucky, I say.

50. The First Year   June 2007

Crikey, we've run this pub for a whole year now. And it hasn't been in the least bit monotonous, trying, frustrating or overwhelmingly exhausting. Hold on. Who am I trying to kid? Of course it has. The struggle to always be at your best, every day of the week, is relentless. I am tired, both physically and mentally and have honestly never endured anything so difficult in all my life. Even childbirth is easier because at least it's over after a few hours.

That's not to say though, in a strange sort of way, I do feel quite pleased with myself. Against the odds, both Rob and I have stuck at it and clung on (at times with tenacity of limpets on a rock) through the strife, the strain, the worry, the vagaries of customers and the challenges of staff. We have endured the journey so far, dealing with everything from cows to corpses, and have arrived at this point, if not better individuals, then at least thinner ones. And that's not altogether a bad thing.

Ah, but have I enjoyed myself as well? Now, that's a very hard question to answer. Admittedly, I haven't hated every minute of it. Seeing Rob standing on a chair with his arm around Maurice whilst the two of them caterwauled. That made me laugh. Knowing that I can at last pull a pint and, quite surprisingly, understand completely what Rob was talking about on our first day when he kept saying "get a feel for the beer". That pleases me. Actually, I'm so in tune now with the state of the real ale, I can tell if the barrel's about to end, just by one pull on the beer pump.

And that's not the only thing I've learnt. I can change a barrel with my eyes shut (although this is not usually necessary) and I also know that a soft spile is a wooden peg driven into a settling cask to let the air out, because ale carries on fermenting even when its poured. I know ullage refers to waste beer and fobbing refers to any lager or beer that is overly frothy (though, why on earth they need new words to describe this is anyone's guess. What's wrong with 'waste' and 'frothy'? Perfectly good words in their own right and, more crucially, everyone knows what they actually mean).

I understand now how to organise a busy restaurant and can waitress-serve around 40 people in one night, all on my own. I can calculate gross profit margin on food at the drop of a hat and if push really does come to shove I can even chargrill a steak for a paying customer (only if they want a well done steak, mind you).

I've discovered I can break up a fight without getting punched myself and I now know that no matter how difficult and insurmountable a situation may seem, there's always a solution (although I never want to go through the stress and anxiety of dealing with an employee like our first chef, ever again).

Besides all that, the most significant lesson I've learnt, and here's a curious thought, is that all those customers - the regular ones, the infrequent ones, the summer ones, the difficult ones, the interesting ones, the boring ones, the pissed ones - are really what this business is all about. Don't get me wrong, the customers can bring you joy or take you to the depths of despair, but no matter how they make you feel they are the sole reason why you work so hard. Without all the customers, running a pub is just a series of pointless daily tasks. And whilst I know we've spent a lot of time knocking them over the past year, I do realise I need the customers way more than they need me and I'm honestly grateful and more than honoured they come to my pub, even if they do rub us up the wrong way on many occasions.

Yes customers figure largely in your life if your life is all about the pub trade and, apart from a purpose and a livelihood they've also given me many a good laugh and no-end of good gossip. A year down the line I am astonished to realise customers are really important and I hold every single one of them in very high regard (even the awkward and demanding ones).

I'm also quite chuffed at my newfound ability to remain calm in sticky situations (except those involving poo). And staying on the pleasing subject of how great I am, I find it staggering the sheer amount of stamina I have, which has never manifested itself in my life prior to this year. And how polite, jolly and welcoming I can be night after night after night (despite Rob's grumpiness). I never thought I had so much staying power. It's astounding to me how long I can stand behind the bar and listen to that boring chap tell me his dry opinions on tarmac, loose shale or gravel.

It's also extremely gratifying that now, at long last, we have been able to put some of our crowd-pulling ideas into practice. Since the new chef arrived in February we've had a 'mussels, chips and beer' night and a comedy night. We've introduced groceries and a book club and all the bed and breakfast owners in the area have been invited to dinner on us, to sample our food so they can recommend the pub to their customers. We've lured the local branch of Young Farmers here from another pub (they meet once a fortnight and there's usually about 30 or 40 of them each time). We've had an auction of promises that raised over £1,000 for the cricket club and had numerous press releases in the local newspaper promoting the pub and our new activities.

Yes, it's not all been bad. I wouldn't rush to do this again if I had the choice, but I can grudgingly say that facing your challenges squarely in the face day after day and then finding a way to solve them is extremely satisfying. And if you can call that enjoying yourself, then I have to admit I have. That's not to say I'm unconcerned about it all. As you know, it's a fine balance between exceeding your customer's expectations and pissing them off completely. I worry myself sick, every time I open the front door, will we make some money today? What is also of concern is just how long can Rob and I keep up this level of frenetic activity? Whilst I now know what I'm doing, more or less, it doesn't mean there are fewer things to do. Surely, at some point our stamina will run out. But you just can't stop. Ever. Because, after all, in the pub trade you're only as good as your customers' last meal.

Still, it's our first year anniversary, isn't it? And I put aside my concerns in order to have a party to mark the occasion. Looking at it now, the morning after the night before, I can honestly say it was a blast. We had a great time.

We decided to have a live band and, because we know someone in the village who plays in one, we asked him if he'd do us the great favour of providing the music for our anniversary bash. We also decided to serve some free food, passing bits and pieces around the pub at regular intervals.

I dug out a dress I'd saved from the days when we had a proper life and wore that instead of my usual blouse and trousers combo and I was either brave or foolhardy enough to also wear heels as I thought the occasion (and the dress) demanded it. I managed to last all night without my feet hurting too much, so that was ok. It was a Friday night and we were absolutely full to the brim with people. They were everywhere, even spilling out on to the road at the front and into the garden at the back. There were more people in the pub than there'd been at any other point during the year. More people than on Christmas Day and New Year's Eve and the amazing thing is, I knew everyone of them.

I'd made sure we had enough staff working so Rob and I didn't have to be behind the bar too much and I spent a very pleasant time socialising with and circulating amongst all the people who were enjoying themselves. So many people wanted to talk to me, it was a bit like being a famous movie star but without the huge earnings and the popping camera flashes. Things were going so well, that later on we cleared a small area near the band and people started to dance. One of our young customers was dancing with Maurice's mum. What was most surprising and heart warming about this was, not that the young and old were dancing together, but that Maurice had bought his mum out to our pub for the evening. He'd never done it before. In fact he'd never even mentioned her in the last year. I didn't even know his mum was still alive.

It was all good. But I still can't shake off the feeling we're living on a knife-edge. The licensed trade is so shaky and I constantly worry where the next pound is coming from. As I've said before, it takes a long time to build a reputation and a short time to lose it. Thankfully, there do not appear to be any repercussions from 'poogate'. How lucky we are.

Nevertheless, we've managed to survive a year already, which is an achievement, surely? And because of that I was determined to enjoy myself last night, to forget my anxieties and concerns for the future and live it up a little in the here and now. So, I settled down to listen to the band play their first set. Due to concern for the neighbours we'd asked for something acoustic, something settling and calming, something soft and laid back something REM or Norah Jones style. They launched straight into Paranoid by Black Sabbath. I ask you, is my state of mind that transparent?

Lightning Source UK Ltd.
Milton Keynes UK
UKOW051653100412

190409UK00001B/20/P